THE DECADES OF TWENTIETH-CENTURY AMERICA

★ ★ ★ ★ ★ ★ ★ ★ ★ ★ ★ ★ ★ ★ ★ ★ ★ ★

AMERICA IN THE 1970s

★ ★ ★ ★ ★ ★ ★ ★ ★ ★ ★ ★ ★ ★ ★ ★ ★ ★

MARLEE RICHARDS

Twenty-First Century Books · Minneapolis

To RBB, my resource, second editor, and support

Twenty-First Century Books
A division of Lerner Publishing Group, Inc.
241 First Avenue North
Minneapolis, MN 55401 U.S.A.

Website address: www.lernerbooks.com

Library of Congress Cataloging-in-Publication Data

Richards, Marlee.
    America in the 1970s / by Marlee Richards.
        p.   cm. — (The decades of twentieth-century America)
    Includes bibliographical references and index.
    ISBN 978–0–8225–3438–9 (lib. bdg. : alk. paper)
    1. United States—History—1969—Juvenile literature. 2. Nineteen seventies—Juvenile literature. I. Title. II. Title: America in the nineteen seventies.
    E855.B74 2010
    973.924—dc22   2007038570

Manufactured in the United States of America
1 2 3 4 5 6 – PA – 15 14 13 12 11 10

CONTENTS

★ ★ ★ ★ ★ ★ ★ ★ ★ ★ ★ ★ ★ ★ ★ ★

★ ★ ★ ★ ★ ★ ★ ★ ★ ★ ★ ★ ★ ★ ★ ★

President JOHN F. KENNEDY shakes hands with PEACE CORPS VOLUNTEERS in the 1960s.

THE TIMES THEY ARE A-CHANGIN'

Change and hope marked U.S. life in the 1960s. The economy was strong, and families thrived. The time seemed right for experimenting.

On the national level, Americans elected their youngest president ever in 1960. At forty-three years old, John Kennedy was smart, handsome, and stylish. His glamorous wife and two small children embodied the ideal youthful U.S. family. Kennedy's platform focused on the future. He proposed bold new ideas for the United States.

At his 1961 inauguration, President Kennedy challenged the nation. "My fellow Americans," he said, "ask not what your country can do for you—ask what you can do for your country." Within weeks, he created the Peace Corps, a government program that trained young volunteers to aid people in poor nations. Kennedy's relatives—many of whom were also powerful in government, business, and society—shared his thirst for change. His sister Eunice Kennedy Shriver founded the Special Olympics. This sports competition encouraged athletes with disabilities to shine in a society that preferred them out of sight. The president's brother Robert Kennedy championed racial and economic justice.

Change occurred in ordinary neighborhoods too. Groups of people who suffered prejudice pushed for equal rights. African Americans fought for the right to eat, travel, and learn in the same places as people of other races. To a great extent,

African Americans carry signs for equal rights while attending the 1963 **MARCH ON WASHINGTON**. There, Martin Luther King Jr. delivered his "I have a dream" speech.

they won this right—but at a price. The 1960s saw many black activists and their supporters suffer beatings, jail, and even death. By the end of the 1960s, segregation (enforced separation of blacks and whites in public places) became illegal. But much work remained to break down the long-standing social walls segregation had built.

Women, too, found their collective voice during the 1960s. Many marched in the streets to demand the right to participate in the same activities as men. The birth control pill (often called the Pill) expanded life choices available to women. Females could finally control if and when they had children. Five million women used the Pill within five years of its introduction in 1960. Many of these women seized the freedom from

unplanned pregnancy to delay marriage and motherhood and join the workforce. They battled to enter professions and land jobs once off-limits to females.

Among all races and both sexes, young people called the loudest for change during the 1960s. The U.S. birthrate had spiked after World War II (1939–1945), resulting in a huge— and young—population. Sociologists called this spike in births from 1946 to 1964 a baby boom. By the mid-1960s, 40 percent of Americans were younger than seventeen.

Some baby boomers challenged their parents, government, and society. They pressed for an alternate culture that embraced experimentation. With their sheer numbers, this group of boomers, often called hippies, stretched social norms in every aspect of life—work, living arrangements, the arts, and more. Their mantra was "Do your own thing." Folksinger Bob Dylan's 1964 release "The Times They Are a-Changin'" became their theme song. The song's lyrics told the older generation to step aside—because young people were about to change the world.

Hippies danced to rock-and-roll music, grew their hair long, and dressed in casual, colorful clothing. They hung popular fluorescent posters reading "Peace, love, and rock and roll." Their bell-bottoms, brightly painted vans, mind-altering drugs, and free love (sex without commitment) caused great concern among more traditional folks.

■ HAWKS AND DOVES

Traditionalists and hippies alike were mostly positive in the early 1960s. But by the end of the decade, rage mounted over the Vietnam War (1957–1975). The nation split over how to manage this prolonged struggle in Southeast Asia.

The United States had been involved in Vietnam since the 1950s. President Harry Truman (who served in office from 1945 until 1953) sent military aid to help France battle Communist rebels there. Vietnam was then a French colony, or dependent territory, as were its neighbors, Laos and Cambodia.

Western countries, such as France and the United States, feared the spread of Communism. Communists wanted to distribute a nation's riches equally and abolish private property. Under Communism individuals give up not only personal wealth but also personal freedoms, such as religion and voting rights, for the good of the community. In Communist nations, people cannot own their own businesses or homes, elect their own leaders, or make their own decisions. Most Americans disagreed with Communism.

France granted all its Southeast Asian colonies independence by 1954. The French pullout left Vietnam divided into Communist North Vietnam and non-Communist South Vietnam. The United States supported South Vietnam because lawmakers believed North Vietnam had set its sights on expansion. In the 1950s, Truman's successor, Dwight Eisenhower, sent money and military advisers to bolster anti-Communist governments in Southeast Asia. In the 1960s, Eisenhower's successors, Kennedy and Lyndon Johnson, added other forms of assistance. Kennedy sent 16,000

U.S. troops to Vietnam. By 1968 Johnson had increased that number to 550,000.

The growing war alarmed young men eligible for the draft (required military service). About the same time, a string of political murders destroyed the hope and trust of many Americans in their government. Dozens of U.S. civil rights workers had died for their efforts. In 1963 an assassin killed President Kennedy. In 1968 civil rights activist Martin Luther King Jr. and Robert Kennedy were also killed.

Disillusioned Americans protested the Vietnam War. These protesters—often called doves—marched, rioted, and sang. All these activities expressed doves' desire to end the war and bring U.S. troops home.

But plenty of Americans still supported U.S. involvement in Vietnam. These hawks not only agreed with the war but also sought a more stable nation. They watched in horror as some antiwar demonstrations turned violent. Hawks wondered if the nation would ever recover.

■ A NEW PRESIDENT

In late 1968, Richard Nixon narrowly defeated Hubert Humphrey to become U.S. president. Voters saw Nixon as someone who could calm the troubled nation. During his campaign, he had promised to restore law and order. He had also promised to end the Vietnam War quickly.

Shortly after Nixon took office in 1969, however, he ordered planes to bomb Cambodia and Laos. Both countries claimed to be neutral. But they let Vietnamese Communists operate freely within their borders. Nixon's move worried Congress. He'd neither warned them nor asked for their approval for the bombings.

In November 1969, journalists broke a disturbing news story. In 1968 U.S. soldiers had massacred hundreds of civilians at My Lai, a village in South Vietnam. Top military officers had covered up the act. The world was outraged. To reduce dissent, Nixon continued the troop withdrawal begun in July 1969. By year's end, 115,000 soldiers left Vietnam, but 515,000 remained. Nixon also established a draft lottery to make military selection fairer.

■ MAKE LOVE, NOT WAR

As more lies surfaced, young people realized the need to protest for peace. Students across the nation burned draft cards and U.S. flags. Many disrupted college and government activities. Most opposition, however, was peaceful. In March 1969, Beatles band member John Lennon married artist Yoko Ono. They used the event to call attention to world suffering and violence. The newlyweds hosted a honeymoon "bed-in for peace" in the Hilton in Amsterdam. The press pursued them, assuming the famous nudist couple would make love for their cameras. Instead, Lennon and Ono lounged in their pajamas and gave interviews that spread their message of peace to a global audience.

In July the eyes of the world focused on a different American. Televisions around the globe showed U.S. astronaut Neil Armstrong stepping onto the moon. Armstrong was the first human to set foot anywhere besides on Earth. His twenty-one hours on the moon amazed the world and lifted U.S. spirits. The United States had grave problems to solve. But if it could put a man on the moon—a feat deemed impossible just a few years earlier—surely the country could find a way to make peace on Earth.

One month later, an all-star cast of folk and rock musicians performed antiwar and other songs at the

JOHN LENNON AND YOKO ONO allowed photographers to capture their 1969 honeymoon at a Hilton hotel in Amsterdam, Holland, in an effort to promote peace.

largest outdoor rock concert to date. The Woodstock Music and Art Fair took place on a farm in Bethel, New York. Four hundred thousand young people arrived for three days of groovy entertainment. The audience listened, danced, did drugs, made love, and slept outdoors in the rain. But no violence occurred. Like an earlier love-in in San Francisco, this event attracted considerable press coverage. People across the nation hoped Woodstock was the beginning of the end of riotous clashes.

PRESIDENT RICHARD NIXON, during a televised address in April 1970, describes his plan to send troops into Cambodia.

CHAPTER ONE

THE NIXON YEARS:
POLITICS AND POLICY IN THE EARLY 1970s

The brief calm inspired by the Woodstock festival shattered in the spring of 1970. On April 30, President Nixon gave a televised address announcing his decision to invade Cambodia. The news left voters feeling betrayed. Nixon seemed to be reversing the U.S. Vietnamization policy. According to this policy, the United States would train the South Vietnamese army to take over, so U.S. troops could return home. Nixon's announcement meant that thirty-one thousand U.S. soldiers would transfer from Vietnam to Cambodia.

HELL NO, WE WON'T GO!

Within hours of Nixon's broadcast, war protesters rushed into the streets. Violent demonstrations erupted at five hundred U.S. campuses. At Kent State University in Ohio, the National Guard killed four students and wounded many more.

After this incident, students at colleges, universities, and high schools throughout the nation organized in anger. They forced administrators to close down hundreds of schools nationwide. They walked out, blocked entrances, or refused to leave classrooms—sometimes for several days. Buses carrying protesters of all ages flooded into Washington, D.C. Anxious troops guarded the White House against rioters.

The White House and many government officials offered no sympathy for the dead and injured protesters. Hawks hated being questioned, believing protests strengthened U.S. enemies by showing that the country was divided. Many lawmakers had fought in World War II. These veterans saw military service—regardless of the cause—as a patriotic duty. Ronald Reagan (then California's governor) responded to a similar action against student protesters in Berkeley by saying, "If it takes a bloodbath [to suppress them], let's get it over with."

As protests escalated, many soldiers in Vietnam lost their will to fight. Popular support for the war was fading, but soldiers were still stuck in danger. Moreover, winning seemed beyond their reach. U.S. troops fought an enemy they could not see in an unfamiliar landscape. As soldiers patrolled Vietnam's steamy swamps and rice paddies without roads or markers, they became easy prey to local enemies who knew the terrain.

> ## "If it takes a bloodbath, let's get it over with."
>
> *—Ronald Reagan, April 7, 1970, responding as California's governor to student protesters in Berkeley*

A SOLDIER IN VIETNAM expresses his desire for peace.

n Kent, Ohio, four days of chaos followed news of the U.S. invasion of Cambodia. The students at Kent State University organized a series of peaceful demonstrations, but some angry participants (including local nonstudent citizens) grew destructive. On May 1, 1970, more than one hundred rioters overturned cars, broke windows, and spray-painted storefronts in downtown Kent.

The next day, Governor James Rhodes sent the National Guard into Kent to restore order. When the Guard arrived, Kent State's vacant, boarded-up Reserve Officers' Training Corps (ROTC) building was burning. Rhodes called protesters "the worst type of people that we harbor in America."

On May 3, some students tried to help clean up downtown. Frightened citizens pressured the mayor to order a curfew. The Guard forcefully dispersed that evening's rally.

One day later, however, protesters reassembled on campus. This time, when guardsmen tried to disperse them, they threw rocks and refused to leave. Nervous guards shot tear gas into the crowd. One said he heard a gunshot. He fired his rifle wildly at the unarmed students. Screaming and shoving broke out as students scattered. A volley of shots from other guards followed. After the smoke cleared, four students lay dead. Another nine scrambled away injured.

"I cannot overemphasize how much we loved our country and how dismayed, frightened, disgusted we were at the turn of events. . . . I never believed our government would kill us. Once they did . . . we all woke up fast. . . . No longer was the administration something that needed correcting: they needed to be removed," wrote author and antiwar advocate Rita Mae Brown.

13

Mary Ann Vecchio, a protester at KENT STATE UNIVERSITY, anguishes over the body of student Jeffrey Miller. Miller was shot by the Ohio National Guard during antiwar demonstrations in May 1970.

Vietnam veterans, some in wheelchairs, march in an **ANTIWAR PROTEST** in 1971.

Soldiers merely wanted to stay alive until they could leave. Some refused orders, rebelled against their officers, or deserted. The number of soldiers who deserted jumped from 1.5 percent in 1966 to 5.2 percent in 1970. Many soldiers took drugs to help them cope with the horrors of combat. By one officer's account, about sixty-five thousand U.S. soldiers used drugs at some time during their service in Vietnam.

Some soldiers joined Vietnam Veterans Against the War after they came home. All returning soldiers faced a nation that couldn't separate soldiers from bad decisions made by officials. Too often, soldiers came home to find their communities angry at them for doing their duty. Neither U.S. citizens nor their government offered support or understanding of what soldiers had endured.

■ PROBLEMS AT HOME

As the war dragged on, Nixon worried about constant news leaks from his administration. The president asked J. Edgar Hoover, Federal Bureau of Investigation (FBI) director, to eliminate the problem. Hoover suggested taping telephone conversations of officials in the administration. Other presidents had spied on their staff. Nixon, however, taped more conversations of more aides than any president before him. The recordings made in Nixon's office beginning in February 1971 became known as the White House Tapes.

In June 1971, the *New York Times* published portions of the Pentagon Papers. These documents, commissioned by the U.S. Defense Department, reported the true history of U.S. involvement in Vietnam from 1945 to 1967. Among other things, the report revealed U.S. involvement in the 1963 assassination of South Vietnam's president, Ngo Dinh Diem. In addition, the report described government lies to the public about the war. Daniel Ellsberg, a high-level researcher, switched his stance from pro-war to antiwar while working on this project. He later released the report to the press.

At first, the Nixon team relished its publication. The report embarrassed Democrats who had governed before Nixon. Then Nixon began to fear the accounts would increase antiwar cries. He worried that future leaks could damage his own political future.

In July Nixon created a secret unit "to stop the leaks whatever the cost." Members of this unit became known as the Plumbers after their leader hung a sign on his office door reading "David R. Young/Plumber." The Plumbers answered to Nixon and his inner circle only. They used break-ins and wiretaps (telephone recordings) to prevent news leaks and plumb, or search for, useful information. One of their first jobs involved a burglary at the office of Daniel Ellsberg's psychiatrist. Nixon wanted to discredit the man who had revealed the truth about Vietnam by trying to show that Ellsberg was mentally unstable. Nixon justified the Plumbers' illegal activities in the name of national security.

DANIEL ELLSBERG, a researcher for the Pentagon Papers, speaks to the press in 1971.

Richard Nixon was a deeply suspicious and insecure man. He kept his thoughts to himself and trusted few advisers.

Nixon built his political career on fear-mongering and battling Communism. During his 1950 California senatorial campaign, he smeared his opponent, U.S. Representative Helen Gahagan Douglas, as a Communist. Nixon said, among other things, that she was "pink [Communist] right down to her underwear." Douglas responded by dubbing him Tricky Dick. Nixon won the race, but the nickname followed him throughout his career.

As Eisenhower's vice president from 1953 to 1961, Nixon continued his assault on real and imagined Communists. But even his reputation as a Communist buster couldn't win him the 1960 presidential race against John Kennedy. Two years later, he lost another race, this one for California governor, to Edmund "Pat" Brown. After that election, Nixon snarled at reporters: "You won't have Nixon to kick around anymore, because, gentlemen, this is my last press conference." Everyone figured Nixon's political career was over.

Nixon's interest in politics bounced back with the 1968 presidential race. But his distrust of others continued into his presidency. When he entered the White House, he found long-standing professional civil servants carrying out government business without regard to politics. Nixon wanted officials loyal to him leading major departments, regardless of their qualifications. He advocated shrinking the number and scope of government jobs, especially social service projects. Many called Nixon the Imperial President because, like royalty, he was detached from the public and other branches of government.

In August Nixon's aides started keeping an enemies list. The list named anyone judged a threat to Nixon's administration. It included television and newspaper reporters, politicians, labor leaders, entertainers, and university and corporate leaders. The list started with twenty names and grew to more than thirty thousand. Nixon's aides used wiretaps, tax audits, and other forms of government harassment to torment people and organizations on the list.

Nixon was deeply suspicious and obsessed with keeping power. He disregarded Congress, the courts, and even his political party. Yet no one in the White House told Nixon when he was wrong.

◼ REFOCUSING FOREIGN POLICY

To boost his ailing presidency, Nixon made a daring foreign policy move. In 1972 he became the first U.S. president to visit Communist China. Nixon signed a trade agreement that opened Chinese markets for U.S. businesses. This agreement helped contain the Soviet Union's power in Asia because it tipped the power balance between China and the Soviet Union. The Soviet Union (which included Russia and fourteen other republics) was an enemy of both China and the United States.

By midyear Henry Kissinger, the U.S national security adviser, had arranged a presidential trip to Moscow, the Soviet capital. Soviet leaders agreed to a meeting because they feared a U.S.-China alliance. But they disapproved of U.S. bombing in North Vietnam, so they didn't want to appear too friendly. Kissinger assured them the discussions would reach beyond the Vietnam War and benefit both nations. The Soviet Union would gain economic help and a way to thaw its relations with China. Nixon would get a political boost before the 1972 elections.

Pat and Richard Nixon and a crowd of onlookers pose for a picture at the **GREAT WALL OF CHINA** in 1972.

In May 1972, Nixon met with Soviet Communist Party leader Leonid Brezhnev in Moscow. Nixon was the first U.S. president to visit the Soviet Union since World War II. This meeting began a new era in U.S.-Soviet relations.

The men agreed on limiting military buildup to strengthen their weak economies. The Strategic Arms Limitation Treaty (SALT) froze the number of nuclear missiles each nation stockpiled. The SALT didn't stop the arms race, but it opened the door to a safer world. The leaders decided to open trade between their nations and discussed sharing technology.

Although Nixon worked to limit Soviet arms, his administration increased weapons in several other countries. In mid-1972, Nixon advocated reducing U.S. military commitments around the globe. He wanted other nations—not just the United States—to contain their Communist neighbors. To this end, he arranged to sell U.S. weapons to countries such as Iran, Portuguese West Africa (modern Angola), and South Africa. During Nixon's presidency, overseas arms sales increased from one or two billion dollars per year to ten billion dollars per year.

Russian president **LEONID BREZHNEV** *(left)* and **NIXON** *(right)* exchange smiles during their 1972 meeting in Moscow to discuss arms reduction.

Presidential candidate **GEORGE MCGOVERN** speaks to a crowd while on the campaign trail with his family in 1972.

■ THE 1972 ELECTION

The Democratic Party nominated Senator George McGovern of South Dakota to run against Nixon in 1972. Though McGovern was a decorated World War II veteran and an experienced public servant, he never stood a chance. His bold antiwar views scared moderate voters and opened him to unfair Republican assaults. Nixon's propaganda machine turned McGovern into a "champion of amnesty [for men who had illegally avoided the draft], acid [for wanting to legalize marijuana], and abortion [a growing hot-button issue]."

Nixon's administration employed other dirty tricks. On June 17, 1972, the Plumbers broke into the Democratic National Committee headquarters at the Watergate complex in Washington, D.C. Police caught five men there with a suitcase full of dollar bills. None would tell why they were there or who paid them. The administration claimed the botched break-in was a petty burglary.

Luckily for Nixon, most Americans agreed—or never even heard of the break-in before the election. Nixon won 70 percent of the popular vote, more than any earlier president. He bested McGovern in every state except Massachusetts.

Instead of celebrating his victory, Nixon grew insecure. Kissinger noticed that as poll results came in, "Nixon withdrew ever more, even from his close advisers. His resentments, usually so well controlled, came increasingly to the surface. It was as if victory was not an occasion for reconciliation, but an opportunity to settle the scores of a lifetime."

Nixon had fooled the nation and beaten back his enemies—but not for long. He couldn't stop further investigation of the Watergate break-in. Authorities had arrested two more suspects in the case. A federal court tried and convicted all seven men in January 1973. The trial revealed that the men were employees of the Committee to Reelect the President (CREEP). Many people suspected that Nixon's administration was involved in the burglary and was trying to cover it up. Both Congress and the press mounted a major inquiry.

> **" It was as if victory was not an occasion for reconciliation, but an opportunity to settle the scores of a lifetime."**
>
> *—Henry Kissinger, recalling President Nixon's reaction to winning the 1972 presidential election*

The Senate created a committee to investigate the Watergate break-in. Soon one of the burglars broke his silence. He admitted that John Mitchell, attorney general and head of Nixon's reelection campaign, had organized the burglary.

Two young *Washington Post* reporters, Bob Woodward and Carl Bernstein, sniffed at the trail linking the Plumbers with CREEP and the White House. They received help from a secret FBI informer who called himself Deep Throat. Woodward and Bernstein wrote a series of almost two hundred articles exposing abuse of power at the highest levels of government. As the stories appeared,

In 1973 writers for the *Washington Post* **CARL BERNSTEIN** *(left)* and **BOB WOODWARD** *(right)* published articles about the Watergate break-in.

AMERICA IN THE

Secretary of State Henry Kissinger *(right front)* shakes hands with North Vietnamese leader Le Duc Tho in 1973 after signing the **PARIS PEACE ACCORDS** ending the war in Vietnam.

Nixon kept denying knowledge of the Watergate break-in or burglars.

■ VIETNAM WAR ENDS

Meanwhile, U.S. involvement in Southeast Asia was winding down. On January 27, 1973, the United States, North Vietnam, South Vietnam, and South Vietnamese Communist rebels signed the Paris Peace Accords. Fighting in Vietnam stopped immediately. Sixty days later, U.S. soldiers and released prisoners of war left Vietnam. Some advisers stayed behind to help with the transition.

The United States continued bombing Cambodia into the summer. By then North and South Vietnam had resumed fighting each other. The U.S. draft officially ended in April. By mid-August, all U.S. guns in Southeast Asia fell silent.

About 3.4 million U.S. soldiers served in Southeast Asia. Of these, 58,177 died, 153,303 returned wounded, and more than 2,000 were still missing. About 20,000 to 30,000 U.S. soldiers and men of draft age followed a modern Underground Railroad into Canada to avoid the draft. Up to 125,000 Americans moved to Canada to protest the Vietnam War.

Few returning soldiers received the hero's welcome given to veterans of earlier wars. They struggled to reenter their families and communities. Many suffered mental health problems. Others had unusual physical symptoms. Yet the government refused to acknowledge their trauma or admit that their symptoms resulted from chemical sprays U.S. forces had used to clear the jungle of vegetation.

■ NIXON'S DOWNFALL

President Nixon basked in the glow of ending the longest war in U.S. history. Americans heaved a sigh of relief. But these good feelings proved brief. Throughout 1973 and 1974, the Watergate plot unraveled, angering Americans of all ages and ideals.

One by one, Nixon's aides resigned after admitting illegal activities. They confessed to payoffs, bribes, robbery, wiretaps, and illegal use of campaign funds. As the investigation continued, some destroyed evidence. The nation watched in horror as the probe crept closer to the president. Nixon still claimed he knew nothing.

In summer 1973, John Dean, White House counsel (lawyer to the president), told the Senate committee that Nixon had ordered payments to quiet the Watergate robbers. Three weeks later, the committee discovered that Nixon had audiotapes of conversations that would prove Dean's charges. Nixon fought to keep five hundred tapes and documents from the Senate committee. He claimed that national security was at stake. When his protests failed, he fired the special prosecutor (the attorney leading the investigation) and sued in court to keep the tapes secret.

As the plot unfolded, another White House case captured national attention. Vice President Spiro Agnew resigned after pleading guilty to bribery and tax violations committed when he was governor of Maryland. Nixon nominated the House of Representatives' Republican leader, Gerald Ford, to replace Agnew. In December 1973, Congress approved Nixon's choice.

By March 1974, the Senate committee charged seven former White House staff members, called the Watergate Seven, with obstructing the Watergate investigation. Four months later, the Supreme Court ordered Nixon to turn over his tapes to Leon Jaworski, the new special prosecutor. This was the Supreme Court's first criminal decision against a president.

At first Nixon offered written transcripts, but the committee refused. After Nixon handed over the tapes, the

RICHARD NIXON makes his famous victory sign as he boards a helicopter on the White House lawn after resigning from the presidency in 1974.

committee discovered an eighteen-and-a-half-minute gap in a key conversation. The exchange on the gap remained a mystery.

Nonetheless, the testimonies and tapes destroyed the president. Nixon lost his support in Congress. In July 1974, the House Judiciary Committee approved three articles to impeach the president (charge him with misconduct). These articles charged him with obstruction of justice, abuse of power, and contempt of Congress.

Realizing he'd finally lost, Nixon spared himself and the nation the ordeal of an impeachment trial. Broken and isolated, Nixon announced his resignation on August 8, 1974. As stunned television viewers watched, he admitted only mistakes—never guilt.

The next morning, a wounded president said good-bye to his teary White House staff. "Always remember," Nixon said, "others may hate you, but those who hate you do not win unless you hate them—and then you destroy yourself." Former aides accompanied the president and his family to the airport. Before boarding the plane for California, Nixon handed Kissinger, the only member of the president's inner circle untouched by crime, a letter of resignation.

At noon the same day, Gerald Ford took the oath of office and became the nation's thirty-eighth president. Afterward, Ford spoke of healing the "wounds of Watergate." He told the nation: "May our former president, who brought peace to millions, find it for himself."

GERALD FORD *(left)* takes the oath of office to become president of the United States on August 9, 1974.

CHAPTER TWO

UNEASY POSTWAR YEARS:
POLITICS AND POLICY IN THE LATE 1970s

Nixon had shattered the nation's trust in its government. Never before had a U.S. president resigned in disgrace. And never before had anyone become vice president and president, as Ford did, by way of the Twenty-fifth Amendment to the Constitution. (The 1967 amendment outlined succession procedures for both offices.)

Ford turned out to be the perfect healer for a stunned and heartsick nation. Citizens and lawmakers of both parties found him experienced and likable. Ford had easily won twelve elections as a U.S. representative from Michigan. He said, "I felt very confident about my ability to do the job. . . . I had been the [House] Republican leader for nine years; I had dealt firsthand with presidents from Eisenhower to Kennedy to Johnson to Nixon; I had, fortunately, been on committees which were of major consequence in foreign policy and military strategy."

UNTANGLING THE MESS

Ford inherited a mess. Unemployment and prices for goods shot to record highs. Energy shortages threatened businesses and home-owners. Foreign leaders expressed concern about relations with the new U.S. president.

Ford appointed Nelson Rockefeller, a multimillionaire and former New York governor, as his vice president. Ford also chose a new cabinet (group of presidential advisers). But as he'd promised Nixon, Ford kept Kissinger on board as secretary of state. Kissinger provided continuity and experience in foreign relations.

PRESIDENT FORD *(left)* gets advice from **HENRY KISSINGER** *(right)*, whom Ford kept on as secretary of state.

firm. "I felt I had an obligation to spend 100 percent of my time on the problems of 230 million people, rather than 25 percent of my time on the problems of one man," he said.

Eight days after the pardon, Ford announced another effort to heal the nation. He offered draft evaders and military deserters living abroad the opportunity to return home. But they had to sign an oath of allegiance and promise two years of public service. The offer resulted in mixed reviews. It appealed to a general public that wanted the war behind them. But veterans attacked the plan as too forgiving, and antiwar Americans said it implied guilt—which they refused to consider. Only about 20 percent of about fifty thousand eligible men accepted the offer.

Next, Ford moved to calm a public outrage over large corporate campaign contributions during the 1972 elections. Donors to presidential and congressional campaigns expected favors from lawmakers in return for financial

Watergate decisions consumed much of Ford's time and energy during his first month in office. Newspaper headlines focused on past crimes instead of pressing current issues. Ford believed that a long trial for Nixon would cripple the country. So on September 8, 1974, Ford pardoned Nixon for any crimes committed during his presidency.

Critics condemned the pardon. They believed Ford had interfered with the legal process. Some accused him of making a deal with Nixon. But Ford held support. In October 1974, Ford signed a major campaign finance reform bill. The law strictly limited donations to and spending by candidates for federal offices. It also established an independent agency to enforce campaign finance laws.

◼ FOREIGN RELATIONS UNDER FORD

Overall, foreign policy changed little during the Ford administration. Ford focused on relationship building and peacekeeping. He traveled often, trying to satisfy leaders in the Middle East and Asia.

He made little progress in the Middle East. The Arab and Israeli armies clashed constantly. Arab countries had opposed Israel's right to exist since it had become a nation in May 1948. The United States had consistently supported Israel and supplied its military with weapons. That angered Israel's neighbors. In October 1973, Arab nations had embargoed (stopped selling) their oil to the United States and its allies. At the time, the United States bought 35 percent of its oil from Arab nations.

The embargo caused economic chaos in the United States in 1973 and 1974. Gasoline and home-heating oil costs soared. Drivers waited in long lines at gas stations.

For a year and a half, Kissinger shuttled between Israel and Egypt trying to calm tensions in the region. Kissinger traveled so much that reporters dubbed his

Motorists in California line up at the pump during the **GAS SHORTAGE** of the 1970s.

negotiations shuttle diplomacy. He eventually negotiated a cease-fire, but the parties couldn't agree on a final settlement. In March 1975, Kissinger ended negotiations.

President Ford revived talks by inviting leaders from Jordan and Syria into the process. Six months after Kissinger's talks ended, Egyptian president Anwar el-Sadat and Israeli prime minister Yitzhak Rabin signed an agreement that strengthened their cease-fire. The two leaders agreed to settle future differences without military action. Oil was flowing to the United States again. But the Middle East remained a tinderbox.

Conditions in northern Asia remained calm. Ford maintained good relations with China and the Soviet Union. Ford and Brezhnev extended limits on nuclear arms by negotiating the SALT II agreement.

But the scene in Southeast Asia looked grim. North and South Vietnam had resumed fighting just a few months after the 1973 Paris Peace Accords. In late March 1975, a Communist victory seemed inevitable. Many Americans and South Vietnamese began evacuating.

On April 30, 1975, the South Vietnamese government in Saigon (modern Ho Chi Minh City) surrendered to the Communists. The last Americans in Vietnam narrowly escaped by helicopter as Communist soldiers swarmed into Saigon. Hundreds of thousands of South Vietnamese citizens fled by boat. Ships rescued some of the "boat people." Others landed on the shores of neighboring countries. Many thousands died. North and South Vietnam united under Communist rule.

U.S. citizens evacuate Vietnam aboard military helicopters in April 1975 during the **FALL OF SAIGON.**

U.S. MARINES storm the *Mayaguez* to rescue its American crew in May 1975.

On May 12, Cambodia's Communist forces seized a U.S. cargo ship, the *Mayaguez*. Cambodia claimed the *Mayaguez* was on a spy mission, which Ford denied. Ford responded quickly by ordering a raid to recover the ship and crew. He never received word that Cambodia had already released the entire crew. At first, Americans applauded the show of strength and return of the crew. After news came that fifteen U.S. soldiers had died in a needless raid, Ford's political light dimmed.

■ THE 1976 ELECTION

Ford assumed the Republican Party would nominate him to run for president in 1976. But his reputation as a well-meaning bungler complicated a sure vote. Conservative Republicans had never liked Ford's pardon of Nixon or his liberal-leaning vice president, Rockefeller. Ford had calmed a grateful nation. But the public craved more effective leadership.

Ford faced tough competition within his party from Ronald Reagan, who had just finished two terms as California's governor. Ford continued to back Rockefeller for vice president, even as pressure mounted for a different choice. Rockefeller took the lead and announced he would not run for vice president in the upcoming election. Ford chose Senator Robert Dole of Kansas. The new team captured the Republican nomination.

JIMMY CARTER speaks to voters on the campaign trail in 1976.

Ford's Democratic opponent was a little-known politician from Georgia. James (Jimmy) Carter, a born-again Christian, had been a nuclear engineer, a peanut farmer, a state senator, and Georgia's governor. But he lacked national and international experience.

Voters liked the idea of a political outsider. Nixon had never involved Ford in his crimes. However, Ford's pardon strongly linked him with Nixon. Carter ran as a reformer with deep moral values. His homespun, straightforward manner appealed to a country tired of cynical, scandalous Washington politicians. He promised the U.S. public, "I'll never tell a lie."

Carter defeated Ford in a very close race. Carter's running mate, Minnesota senator Walter Mondale, became vice president. Carter was the first Democratic president to carry all states from the Deep South since Andrew Jackson, who served as president from 1829 to 1837.

On January 20, 1977, Jimmy Carter was sworn in as the thirty-ninth U.S. president. He began his inauguration speech by thanking Ford "for all he has done to heal our land."

Afterward, a motorcade carrying the president and his family crept along Pennsylvania Avenue toward the White House. A surprised crowd of well-wishers cheered as Carter and his wife, Rosalynn, left their limousine and walked the route hand in hand—a presidential first. "I felt a simple walk would be a tangible indication of some reduction in the imperial status of the President and his family," wrote Carter in his autobiography.

S hirley Chisholm battled the odds almost from birth. Always tiny for her age, this African American spitfire refused to let her size—or gender or color—get in the way of her goals. As Chisholm aged, she became an outspoken advocate for women and blacks. She battled the "boys' club" that controlled college student council elections. She noticed how blacks refused to challenge whites or question politics as usual for fear of causing trouble.

Born in New York, Chisholm never played by the rules that said you couldn't get ahead if you were female or black. She worked her way from early childhood classroom teacher to city consultant. Then she bucked the system and naysayers to plunge into New York politics. Her campaign slogan, Unbought and Unbossed, spoke volumes about her desire to take a stand whenever necessary. To the surprise of everyone but Chisholm, she became New York state representative and served from 1964 to 1968. She soon gained a reputation for speaking her mind. "Shirley is a nice person," said Kings County Democratic chairman Stanley Steingut. "She's bright, but she doesn't play by the rules of the game."

In 1969 Chisholm won a seat in the U.S. House of Representatives. She was the first African American congresswoman in

SHIRLEY CHISOLM ran for the Democratic presidential nomination in 1972.

192 years of federal government. Chisholm took another long shot in 1972 when she ran for president. Never before had a woman or an African American run for president— and Chisholm was both. Although she did not win, Chisholm's presidential campaign gained her a large following. New Yorkers sent her back to Congress until 1982. Throughout her career, she repeated, "Of my two 'handicaps,' being female put many more obstacles in my path than being black."

" The worst thing you could say to Carter . . . was that it was politically the best thing to do. "

—Vice President Walter Mondale, reflecting on President Carter's distaste for politics

■ A NATION IN SHAMBLES

Like Ford, Carter inherited a troubled nation. The U.S. image at home and abroad was suffering. Shaky relations continued in the Middle East. Prices soared, and the dollar lost value. Family incomes fell. Businesses and cities went bankrupt.

Carter tried to fix the country's problems single-handedly. He allowed no one else to make his decisions. He went out of his way to show that he bowed to no business lobbies or special-interest groups. "The worst thing you could say to Carter . . . was that it was politically the best thing to do," said Mondale.

As a speed-reader, Carter pored over every paper that crossed his desk. He was frugal in word and deed. To conserve public money, he sold the presidential yacht and cut White House salaries. To save energy, he lowered the White House thermostat to 68°F (20°C), installed solar hot water panels, and wore a sweater.

■ CARTER'S SUCCESSES

One of Carter's first presidential acts was to unconditionally pardon draft evaders and military deserters. This pardon allowed both groups to return to the United States without punishment. Ten thousand men accepted the offer. The United States took another step toward healing its war wounds.

Carter had run for office on a promise to improve human rights around the world. To keep that promise, he reduced monetary aid to countries that abused human rights. As a result, the military governments of Brazil, Chile, and Argentina began treating their citizens better. In addition, Carter challenged minority (white)-ruled South Africa to allow all its citizens to vote.

In September 1977, Carter signed two treaties with Omar Torrijos, leader of Panama. In 1903 Panama had granted the United States the right to build and control the Panama Canal. This 48-mile (77-kilometer) artificial channel links the Atlantic and Pacific oceans. The Torrijos-Carter Treaties returned the canal to Panamanian control and guaranteed that the waterway remained neutral and open to U.S. ships permanently.

Carter maintained many of Nixon's and Ford's policies toward China and the Soviet Union. He increased trade with China and finalized a SALT II treaty with the Soviet Union. He championed human rights in both nations. But Carter did little to press the issue. He believed that other issues, such as the threat of nuclear arms buildup, were too great to anger the Soviets.

President Carter's crowning achievement developed from the Middle East conflict. Israel had withdrawn from the West Bank and Sinai Peninsula (territories Israel had captured from Jordan and Egypt). But attacks on Israel had increased from displaced Israeli Arabs and their supporters in neighboring countries. Israel responded by attacking military bases in southern Lebanon.

The situation was about to explode when Sadat offered to visit Israel. Israel's prime minister, Menachem Begin, accepted the offer and invited Sadat to address the Israeli people.

Sadat made history speaking before Israel's Knesset (legislature). His visit to Israel was the first by an Arab official. Some Arabs called Sadat a traitor. But his visit raised the world's hopes that the two sides could work together. Sadat then invited Begin to address the Egyptian people, which he did in the Egyptian town of Ismailya. After this exchange, however, progress stalled.

In September 1978, Carter invited both leaders to Camp David, the presidential retreat in Maryland, to work out their differences. Carter shuttled

JIMMY CARTER *(center)* meets with Egyptian president ANWAR EL-SADAT *(left)* and Israeli prime minister MENACHEM BEGIN in 1978 to discuss the possibility of peace in the Middle East.

> **"For a few hours, all three of us were flushed with pride and good will. . . . We had no idea at that time how far we still had to go."**

—Jimmy Carter, 1978, after successful peace talks with Israeli and Egyptian leaders

between the two men, coaxing them toward compromise. After thirteen days, the leaders finally agreed on a framework for a peace treaty. A few months later, Begin and Sadat returned to the United States to sign a formal agreement. The Israel-Egypt Peace Treaty ended thirty years of fighting and established the first diplomatic relations between Israel and an Arab neighbor.

"For a few hours, all three of us were flushed with pride and good will toward one another because of our unexpected success," wrote Carter. "We had no idea at that time how far we still had to go."

■ CARTER MISFIRINGS

Although Carter's achievement with Israel and Egypt was stunning, he met few of his other goals. His intelligence and integrity could carry him only so far. He was naive to think he could function without political wheeling and dealing. He never became a Washington insider, and this made it hard for him to get things done. He

had no political support, so Congress either watered down or killed much of his plan to improve the economy. And his handling of events elsewhere in the Middle East proved disastrous.

One inconsistency in Carter's human rights program returned to haunt him. For decades the U.S. government had supported Iranian leader Shah Mohammad Reza Pahlavi. The shah (king) ruled cruelly and distributed oil wealth unequally among Iranians. His secret police tortured and imprisoned about fifty thousand Iranians. But the United States needed a friend in the oil-rich region, so it avoided addressing Pahlavi's abuses. The United States backed Pahlavi's dictatorship in exchange for his support of Western ideas. On a visit to Iran, Carter called Iran "an island of stability in one of the more troubled areas of the world."

Government officials of other Arab Middle East countries and Islamic clerics (religious leaders) condemned Pahlavi's Western leanings. Religious leaders within Iran urged their followers to overthrow him. In 1978 Iranians revolted against the shah. He admitted he couldn't calm the growing discontent. The Pahlavi family barely escaped in January 1979. Exiled cleric Ayatollah Ruholla Khomeini returned to Iran and claimed leadership.

Iranians loyal to Khomeini tore through the countryside killing supporters of the shah and destroying anything related to the United States. Khomeini hated U.S. support of the shah and U.S. participation in the Israel-Egypt Peace Treaty. Khomeini said, "Sadat states he is a Muslim. . . . He is not, for he compromises with the enemies of Islam."

To punish the United States and its allies, Khomeini stopped selling Iranian oil to them. The energy crisis expanded. Khomeini and his followers stirred up hatred of Westerners and their culture, which contradicted strict Muslim tradition and strict interpretation of the Quran (the holy book of Islam). Sensing danger, fifteen thousand Americans fled Iran in 1979. But ten thousand stayed, including the U.S. Embassy staff in Tehran.

In November 1979, an angry mob captured dozens of Americans from the embassy. Despite Carter's efforts to free them, fifty-two hostages remained captive in Iran for the next fourteen months.

35

Iranian students scale a wall outside the **U.S. EMBASSY** in Tehran, Iran. The students seized the embassy and took sixty-six Americans hostage. Fifty-two of the hostages were held for fourteen months.

ahlavi (the shah of Iran) was suffering from cancer when he and his family left Iran. They traveled first to Egypt, Morocco, Barbados, and Mexico. Then Pahlavi requested permission to enter the United States for treatment. On October 23, 1979, Carter agreed.

One week later, Khomeini urged his supporters to demonstrate against the United States. Anger at U.S. support of the shah exploded. On November 4, hundreds of Iranian students stormed the U.S. Embassy. They occupied the building and grabbed sixty-six hostages. The protesters taunted the blindfolded hostages and paraded them before television cameras. The students soon released thirteen captives but detained fifty-three. (One of these was released the following year.)

Though Khomeini hadn't directed the embassy takeover, he supported it afterward. The takeover helped Khomeini easily establish a theocracy (government based on religion). Normally the United States would vocally oppose such an action. But with so many U.S. lives in Iranian hands, the United States wouldn't dare anger Khomeini by interfering with his plan. He said, "This action has many benefits. The Americans do not want to see the Islamic Republic taking root. We keep the hostages, finish our internal work, then release them."

Carter tried negotiating release of the hostages, but Khomeini refused. He demanded Carter hand over Pahlavi. Instead, Carter ordered a rescue mission. But the attack failed, killing eight U.S. soldiers. Their deaths doomed Carter's chance of reelection.

In July 1980, Pahlavi died. Diplomats from Algeria used this situation to open new negotiations. Two days before the U.S. presidential elections, Iran agreed to release the hostages. In return, the United States freed Iranian money frozen in U.S. bank accounts and agreed not to intervene in Iran's domestic affairs.

■ THE 1980 ELECTION

Carter ran for president again in 1980. But his failure to revive the U.S. economy and to bring the hostages in Iran home dragged down his candidacy. Carter faced serious competition from Reagan and popular independent candidate John Anderson. Anderson took 7 percent of the popular vote, a large amount for a third-party candidate. Historians believed Anderson took more votes away from Carter than from Reagan because, although Anderson had formerly been a Republican, his positions more closely aligned with the Democrats. This split left Reagan with 51 percent of the votes and Carter with 41 percent. Libertarian Ed Clark took the remaining 1 percent.

Iran held the hostages until Reagan's inauguration day. President Carter stayed up all night before the inauguration hoping to hear word of their release. At noon on January 20, 1981, he went to Reagan's ceremony. Afterward, Carter heard the news he wanted. Khomeini denied Carter the tiniest bit of success.

"These last few days have been among the worst I've ever spent in the White House," Carter wrote.

FREED AMERICAN HOSTAGES return home from Iran after 444 days of captivity.

Students in New York City push brooms in the
city's Union Square during the United States's
first EARTH DAY in April 1970.

CHAPTER THREE

CAN YOU DIG IT?

SCIENCE AND TECHNOLOGY IN THE 1970s

By 1970 U.S. society had become very wasteful. Fast foods and prepackaged dishes provided quick, easy meals. But these foods increased the amount of litter piling up on city streets. Other garbage—some of it poorly made and barely used goods—added to the waste collecting throughout the countryside and in overflowing landfills. Some people began to question what went into the food they ate, the water they drank, and the air they breathed.

■ FOCUS ON THE ENVIRONMENT

The goods Americans produced, used, and discarded threatened the environment. As factories churned out their wares, the process and products often released substances that ruined nearby water, land, and air. Cars, aerosol cans, and plastics gave off polluting chemicals and crammed landfills with materials that would take thousands of years to break down.

Some people—especially those living in dirty, smoggy cities or near landfills or polluted waterways—worried about the world's air and water supply. Others feared that outer space would soon become the United States' garbage can. These worries led concerned citizens to organize the first Earth Day on April 22, 1970. On that day, activists around the nation held teach-ins to help people understand the importance of preserving the environment.

1970s

40

AMERICA IN THE

Few politicians talked about the environment in 1970. But Gaylord Nelson (1916–2005), U.S. senator from Wisconsin, had been addressing environmental issues throughout his government career. Growing up in Clear Lake, Wisconsin, Nelson developed an appreciation of the nature around him. As Wisconsin's governor (1959–1963), Nelson established a penny-a-pack cigarette tax that went toward preserving state parks, wetlands, and wildlife habitats.

When Nelson became U.S. senator in 1963, the environmental situation outside Wisconsin looked bleak. Pollution in lakes and oceans washed ashore, often closing beaches. Smog choked many cities. Rivers caught fire because they were so polluted. Forests, streams, and open spaces were disappearing, along with plants and animals. Nelson believed saving U.S. natural resources for future generations was Congress's top responsibility. But he was unsure how to convince other lawmakers.

In the summer of 1969, Nelson read about college campuses holding antiwar teach-ins. That September he proposed teach-ins about the importance of preserving the environment. News reporters carried Nelson's vision across the country. His staff ran with the publicity. They planned a nationwide environmental teach-in called Earth Day.

On April 22, 1970, GAYLORD NELSON spoke to a crowd in Denver, Colorado, gathered to celebrate the first Earth Day.

The response was surprising. Congress adjourned (took a break) so members could preside over local Earth Day events. Ten thousand elementary and high schools and two thousand colleges organized activities. Twenty million people across the country celebrated the first Earth Day on April 22, 1970. "On that day," wrote Nelson, "the environment was elected to a permanent position on the national political agenda."

Nelson continued his work for the environment after leaving office in 1980. He served as counselor for the Wilderness Society and spoke on behalf of the environment. In 1995 he received the Presidential Medal of Freedom, a high national honor, for his environmental achievements.

In 1974 President Nixon signed a bill that limited the amount of auto exhaust. Behind him are members of the **ENVIRONMENTAL PROTECTION AGENCY**.

Enthusiastic Earth Day participation showed politicians that ordinary people cared about the environment. As a result, U.S. environmental policy underwent a major transformation. In 1970 President Nixon created the Environmental Protection Agency (EPA). This federal agency replaced the nation's ineffective state environmental programs. The national agency set and enforced national pollution control standards. Several acts flowed from the birth of the EPA and renewed public interest in the environment. By 1973 Congress had passed several laws to control air and water pollution and pesticide damage and to protect marine mammals and other endangered species.

In a major breakthrough, the EPA banned the pesticide dichlorodiphenyl-trichloroethane (DDT). Experts credit the ban with saving several endangered species, including the bald eagle, and reducing many health problems in humans. The ruling banning DDT further required review of all pesticides for cancer causing ingredients.

Environmental legislation continued under the Ford and Carter administrations. Ford, the only president to work as a national park ranger, added eighteen new regions to the national park system. President Ford also signed the Toxic

Substances Control Act into law in 1976, to decrease risks to health and the environment. In 1977 President Carter strengthened air quality standards by signing a major amendment to the 1970 Clean Air Act. By the late 1970s, the effort to clear U.S. skies, lands, and waters was showing signs of success.

But new environmental controls failed to protect the public from decades of past neglect. When misfortune struck the residents of Love Canal, it taught the nation a lesson about environmental dangers.

Love Canal was a 16-acre (6-hectare) abandoned canal near Niagara Falls, New York. Between 1942 and 1952, Hooker Chemical and Plastics used the land to bury more than 21,000 tons (19,051 metric tons) of harmful chemicals in metal barrels there. The city of Niagara Falls covered the land in 1953 and began building a school and homes on it.

Construction broke the canal's clay seal. Through the 1970s, strange odors plagued the neighborhood. Children playing outdoors sometimes came home with burned hands and faces.

After a particularly rainy 1977, the canal's chemicals rose to the surface and spilled into the Niagara River. Even worse, corroded barrels broke through the ground. They appeared in backyards, swimming pools, and basements. An unusually high number of pregnant women miscarried. Those who had babies

In 1978 the U.S. government declared a state of emergency in **LOVE CANAL**, New York. President Carter ordered the Federal Emergency Management Agency to help the city with cleanup efforts. Workers unearthed these tanks holding toxic waste in May 1980.

In 1977 a group of demonstrators wearing T-shirts spelling out **"NO NUKES"** protested at a nuclear power plant in New Hampshire.

saw a disturbing increase in birth defects. Many residents had their blood tested and discovered they had high white blood cell counts. This signaled a greater risk for leukemia (cancer of the blood or bone marrow).

President Carter ordered emergency aid to clean Love Canal and help its residents relocate. The lesson of Love Canal led to the Superfund Act of 1980. This law protects people from abandoned toxic waste sites and holds polluters accountable for their actions.

After Love Canal, people began taking chemical pollution seriously. Since 1974 scientists had been reporting that chlorofluorocarbons (CFCs) were destroying Earth's atmospheric ozone layer. (At the time, CFCs served as propellants, refrigerants, and cleaning solvents.) The ozone layer blocks harmful solar radiation from reaching Earth's surface. Scientists predicted that more exposure to such radiation would increase the risk of cancer in humans. In 1978 the U.S. government banned CFCs.

Many people saw another radiation risk in the nation's nuclear industry. Making nuclear power and nuclear weapons produces radioactive waste. Radiation changes and damages living cells. In humans, radiation increases the risk of nausea, weakness, and various cancers. Radiation alters food, soil, and water sources, endangering people who eat and

> " Blown from the west to east by stratospheric winds, particles [of nuclear waste] descend to the earth by rainfall and work their way through soil and water into the food chain, eventually posing serious threat to human life."

—Helen Caldicott, *Nuclear Madness: What You Can Do*, 1979

drink from these sources. Australian physician Helen Caldicott, who lived in the United States from 1977 until 1986, lectured throughout the country to educate the public about the effects of nuclear radiation on general health and well-being. Her talks warned that "blown from the west to east by stratospheric winds, particles [of nuclear waste] descend to the earth by rainfall and work their way through soil and water into the food chain, eventually posing serious threat to human life." In 1979 she published the book *Nuclear Madness: What You Can Do*. Caldicott's book— as well as her outspoken presence— boosted the antinuclear movement.

■ SPACE EXPLORATION

During the 1970s, citizens hungered for more feats from the space program that had put a man on the moon. They weren't disappointed. The Apollo space program made five more moon landings after *Apollo 11*. The last Apollo moon landing occurred in 1972. But scientists continued to explore the solar system throughout the 1970s via unmanned space missions. As the science of space improved, the Apollo program investigated how space could be adapted to benefit defense and commercial activities.

In 1972 President Nixon announced "the development of an entirely new type of space transportation system designed to help transform the space frontier of the 1970s into familiar territory, easily accessible for human endeavor in the 1980s and 90s." The U.S. space shuttle program was born. Scientists, engineers, and astronauts spent the next nine years preparing for the program's first flight.

The government approved other space programs to explore living and working in space. In 1973 the National Aeronautics and Space Administration (NASA) launched the space station

Skylab. Skylab was an 83-ton (75-metric ton) vessel that carried a crew as it orbited around Earth. The crew studied weightlessness, observed the solar system, took space walks, and conducted scientific and medical experiments.

Back on Earth, ordinary Americans benefited from space studies. Early missions led to development of freeze-dried foods, advances in health care, and better understanding of solar power. As space study continued, scientists developed satellites for communication, navigation, and weather monitoring.

Meanwhile, the United Nations (an international organization that promotes peace and monitors international security and law) established rules to promote peaceful space programs. In 1975 the United States and the Soviet Union cooperated in space for the first time via the Apollo-Soyuz test project. By the end of the decade, both countries permitted astronauts from other nations on space missions. Space exploration was a new way for nations to work together.

In 1975 U.S. astronaut Thomas Stafford *(right)* and Soviet cosmonaut Alexei Leonov *(left)* shake hands in space for the first time during the **APOLLO-SOYUZ TEST PROJECT.**

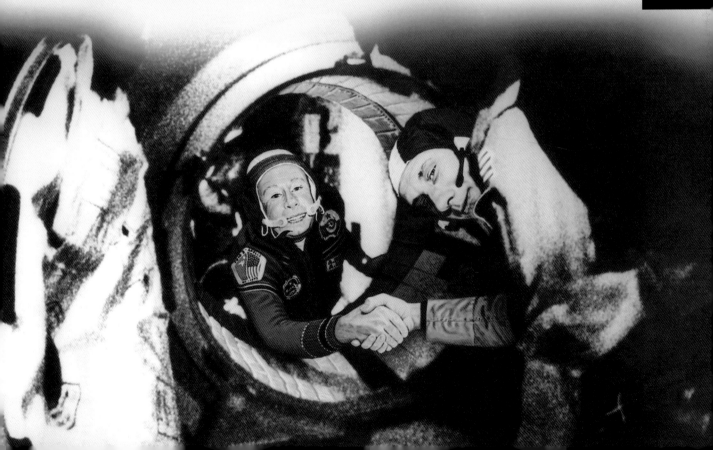

The first Apple computer, **APPLE I**, was sold in 1976 for $666.66. The buyer had to supply a case, power supply, keyboard, and display monitor.

■ SEEDS OF TECHNOLOGICAL CHANGE

Scientists introduced many new technologies during the 1970s. In 1971 Intel released its 4004 chip. The 4004 was the first single device to integrate math, logic, and control circuits that enable a computer to "think." Its tiny size (smaller than a cornflake) let companies produce compact computers instead of the original room-size ones. Invention of the chip led to the birth of the modern computer.

Six years later, Apple announced the first mass-produced personal computers. They were too expensive and difficult to understand for the average family. Some corporations and wealthy individuals bought computers to handle their businesses.

The first electronic desktop calculators had appeared in the 1960s. They were large, heavy business machines that cost thousands of dollars. Portable calculators appeared in 1970. But they still cost hundreds of dollars—too expensive for most individuals.

Pocket-size calculators, computerized record keeping and communication, and wireless technology were years away. Most people kept paper records and communicated by letters sent via the post office. Or they called people on landline telephones. Most phones still operated via circular dials, but touch-tone dialing was gaining popularity.

■ FOOD REVOLUTION

During the 1970s, Americans grew more aware of food's effects on the body. Hippies, environmentalists, and ordinary health-conscious people protested the TV dinners, fast foods, and other highly processed and packaged foods that had grown popular during the 1950s and 1960s.

Instead, they wanted to eat more natural, or organic, foods. These included farm products raised without pesticides, herbicides, or hormones and sold without preservatives or other added chemicals. Advocates of healthy eating championed vegetarian cooking. They developed creative ways to replace meat with other protein foods, such as soy and wheat products, and to prepare tasty meals with vegetables, fruits, whole grains, and legumes (beans and peas). A broader variety of seasonings beyond salt and pepper gained acceptance. As the microwave oven (introduced in 1967) became widely available, cooking healthy food got quicker and easier.

Pediatrician and allergist Ben Feingold added his professional voice to the many others calling for healthier foods in the 1970s. He warned that processed food could cause a host of health and behavior problems. Feingold targeted learning disabilities in particular.

Scientists had studied children with learning disabilities since the 1960s. But how children developed difficulties in processing information remained a mystery. Some researchers believed brain anatomy might explain problems such as dyslexia (a language disability that affects reading and writing) and hyperactivity. But no one knew for sure.

Feingold suspected that in many children, hyperactivity was a reaction to food additives. He singled out artificial flavors, colors, sweeteners, and preservatives. He identified a problematic substance called salicylate in many of these additives as well as in some fruits, vegetables, spices, and nuts. He found that people who avoided food additives and naturally occurring salicylate lost many of their behavior symptoms.

Feingold described his ideas and an additive-free diet in his 1974 book *Why Your Child Is Hyperactive*. Since then other researchers have expanded on his theories.

The food industry and some doctors have challenged Feingold's claims. But scientific research has been generally supportive. And many families have found his diet successful in improving their children's behavior. One thing is certain: Feingold's ideas spurred people to think seriously about what they put in their foods and bodies.

California led the way in flavorful, healthy cooking with natural, seasonal ingredients. Chefs adopted France's lighter version of its traditionally sauce-laden cooking. They called it nouvelle, or new, cuisine. Nouvelle cuisine, vegetarianism, and natural foods soon gained wider audiences on both coasts and in big cities. In the rest of the country, eating changed little. The South kept its barbecue, and most midwesterners preferred red meat and fried foods.

While some people ate more healthfully and others carried on as usual, a growing number saw food as their enemy. U.S. society idealized thinness, especially in women. Many girls starved themselves to look like the scrawny models and celebrities of the decade. As a result, the 1970s ushered in greater public awareness and scientific study of eating disorders.

Some doctors linked eating disorders with fad diets. Some dieters smoked cigarettes or ate only eggs, cabbage, or grapefruit to lose weight. Robert Atkins, a cardiologist (heart doctor), fanned the weight-loss flames with his 1972 book *Dr. Atkins' Diet Revolution*. Atkins advocated losing weight by eating more protein and fat and fewer carbohydrates, including grains, fruits, and vegetables. Critics charged that the diet raised the risk of cancer, heart disease, kidney damage, and osteoporosis (a bone disease). But dieters loved the idea of shedding pounds while feasting on meat, cheese, eggs, and butter. An entire industry grew around Atkins's books and products. Atkins's carefully marketed

ROBERT ATKINS, author of *Dr. Atkins' Diet Revolution*, added to the diet craze of the 1970s with his method for losing weight.

diet brought being thin to center stage. His approach regained popularity for a time in the twenty-first century, and scientists are still hotly debating its safety.

■ PUBLIC HEALTH AND SAFETY

Growing public interest in health and safety led to stronger government protections for workers and consumers. The Occupational Safety and Health Administration (OSHA) formed in 1970. It established and enforced workplace health and safety standards. In 1972 the government established the Consumer Product Safety Commission (CPSC) to protect the public against unreasonable risk of injury or death from consumer products. These agencies required helmets for motorcyclists on interstate highways; established mold reduction guidelines, such as fixing plumbing leaks and ventilating kitchens; and called for food labeling that identified vitamins and minerals. Many consumers began asking questions and reading labels before buying products.

During the 1960s, the U.S. surgeon general (top public health officer) had issued the first government warnings about the health hazards of cigarette smoking. Researchers had found that nonsmokers lived between six and eighteen years longer than smokers. Other research confirmed problems from secondhand smoke. From then on, cigarette companies came under fire. The surgeon general called for tighter tobacco regulations.

Lawmakers grappled with how to convince 37 percent of the adult population to stop smoking and how to prevent all teenagers from starting. In 1971 Congress banned cigarette advertising on television and radio to combat the lure of smoking. To protect nonsmokers from secondhand smoke, smokers and nonsmokers began sitting separately on airplanes and buses in 1973. Four years later, cigars and pipes were banned on planes. State legislators joined the battle too. In 1973 Arizona became the first state to end smoking in public places. By the decade's end, adult tobacco use dropped to its lowest level since 1898.

49

In 1973 Arizona became the first state to end smoking in public places.

A family of four sits in their living room decked out with
THE LATEST FURNISHINGS AND A COLOR TV.

CHAPTER FOUR

THE GREAT ROLLER-COASTER RIDE:
THE 1970s ECONOMY

During the 1950s and 1960s, widespread prosperity had led to a culture of buying. Many Americans had become focused on acquiring possessions. This material lifestyle continued into the 1970s.

SHOP TILL YOU DROP

Many baby boomers entered the workforce and began earning sizable salaries in the 1970s. Although poverty persisted in inner cities and the rural South, average annual incomes had doubled: from $5,600 in 1950 to $12,000 in 1973. Raised in the spirit of consumption, boomers rarely refused to spend money on the latest fads and fashions—even if they didn't have it. Credit cards grew in popularity as a way to postpone payment. Young adults often preferred self-fulfillment over savings. They were willing to take financial risks to achieve material gain.

Bigger was better for 1970s consumers. People not only wanted more stuff, they wanted more noticeable toys: for example, larger televisions and fancier cars. Advertisers and retailers encouraged people to buy more than they needed. Shoppers refused to curb their buying appetites.

In response, companies produced trendy products meant for quick turnover. Manufacturers planned for appliances, clothes, and other goods to wear out fast, so users would need to buy replacements. A 1966 poll of

51

consumers had found that 75 percent of respondents believed U.S. businesses sold good or excellent products. By 1977 another survey revealed that 27 percent of U.S. workers "felt so ashamed of the quality of the goods they made that they would not buy them for themselves."

> " [U.S. workers] felt so ashamed of the quality of the goods they made that they would not buy them for themselves. "

—*David Frum, 1977 consumer poll*

■ A TROUBLED ECONOMY

Although Americans spent money like crazy, the U.S. economy was in trouble. Prices steadily rose (inflation) while the value of U.S. goods and services declined (stagnation). Economists called this situation stagflation.

The Vietnam War endangered the nation's economy. Health-care, education, and public aid programs begun in the 1960s received less government funding in the 1970s because vast sums of money went to the military. Goods needed for the war grew scarce at home. The shortages, in turn, drove up prices.

The Middle East crisis contributed to U.S. economic problems. Arab nations supplied 35 percent of U.S. oil in the 1970s. These nations manipulated the cost and amount of oil they exported to gain leverage over the United States and Western Europe (and by extension, Israel). The high cost and scarcity of oil had little effect on the United States' energy appetite. Americans just spent more money on oil and petroleum-based products, such as gasoline, ink, plastics, fertilizers, and paint. To offset oil costs, companies cut jobs and raised their prices. Unemployment and high prices slowed down U.S. economic activity.

Rising prices made U.S. goods and materials more expensive than those from Japan and Western Europe. To save money, U.S. manufacturers imported more goods and parts from overseas. At one time, the United States had dominated the electronics industry. In the 1970s, U.S. companies began assembling radios, cameras, and televisions—including new color ones—from Asian-made parts.

The U.S. automobile industry had driven the nation's economy for more

IMPORTED CARS fill the port at Baltimore Harbor in Maryland. Baltimore's steel plant sits in the background. Demand for steel in American car manufacturing dropped during the 1970s.

than a half century. But U.S. cars, which were expensive and inferior compared to imported ones, no longer ruled the industry by the 1970s. Japanese cars flooded into the United States. Between 1970 and 1971, the number of Japanese car imports nearly doubled, reaching seven hundred thousand per year. Factory workers and a nervous nation worried about the number of jobs lost to Japan.

■ EFFORTS TO IMPROVE THE ECONOMY

In 1971 President Nixon tried to slow inflation by freezing wages and prices. He added taxes on foreign goods. He hoped higher prices on imports would help U.S. products compete.

The plan worked at first. Nixon managed to calm jittery voters before the 1972 election. But two years later, the U.S. economy slipped again. Nixon removed the freeze, but the damage was done. With the economy faltering, the U.S. image as a superpower suffered. Foreign countries saw the United States managing its economy poorly for the first time since the late 1800s.

	1970s	2000s (first decade)
Average U.S. worker's income	$7,564	$35,000

TYPICAL PRICES

	1970s	2000s
Dozen eggs	61¢	$2.18
Quart of milk	$1.15	$1.79
Loaf of bread	24¢	$2.79
Stamps	6¢	42¢
Movie ticket	$1.55	$9.00
Gallon of gas	36¢	$2.80
Two-door car	$3,900	$20,000
Three-bedroom house	$23,400	$300,000

(Prices are samples only. At any given time, prices vary by year, location, size, brand, and model.)

President Ford hoped to put the economy back on track. He called for a variety of reforms, including tax cuts to encourage buying. He suggested a number of government cost-cutting measures. Both efforts were sorely needed, and both attacked abuses by wealthy individuals and corporations. But critics deemed these efforts "too little too late."

When Carter became president, he added several plans. To balance tax burdens, he proposed the first revision of the income tax code in thirty years. His reforms increased the minimum percentage of income that wealthier people paid. New tax codes also dismantled tax shelters that wealthy businesses and individuals used to avoid paying their fair share.

To address the energy problem, Carter created a new federal Department of Energy. Under his direction, the department investigated other forms of energy, such as wind, solar, and nuclear power as well as synthetic fuels made from natural products. The Carter administration proposed building more nuclear power plants. But after a near-deadly accident occurred at the Three

Mile Island nuclear facility in Pennsylvania, public distrust of nuclear energy increased. Congress imposed new safeguards on the plants in use and ended plans to build more.

Despite these efforts, the economy floundered. Inflation and unemployment soared. Oil started flowing through the new Trans-Alaska Pipeline in 1977. Yet oil prices remained high. Carter lashed out at oil companies for gouging the public.

President Carter visited **THREE MILE ISLAND** in Harrisburg, Pennsylvania, several days after one of the nuclear reactors leaked radiation.

HARE KRISHNAS dance, chant, and play music on a busy street in midtown Manhattan, New York. Several religious groups attracting large memberships cropped up in the 1970s.

CHAPTER FIVE

BATTLE FOR EQUAL RIGHTS:
SOCIAL CHANGE IN THE 1970s

The 1970s were nearly as freewheeling as the 1960s. Many people experimented with nontraditional philosophies, substances, relationships, and living arrangements. Some segments of the population still fought for basic civil rights. Those who disagreed with these changes either tried to cope or worked to limit social change.

■ THE ME DECADE

Many baby boomers shifted their focus inward as they reached adulthood. They were tired of war and protesting to change the world. Some tuned out with marijuana and other illegal drugs.

Other people tried to improve themselves, since improving the planet was too hard. Novelist Tom Wolfe described this trend in an essay about the 1970s titled "The 'Me' Decade and the Third Great Awakening." To satisfy their yearning for self-improvement, many people turned to fad therapies, self-help books, and new religious movements.

Religious groups such as the Hare Krishnas, the Unification Church, and the Peoples Temple attracted large followings in the 1970s. The leaders of such sects had magnetic personalities and appealing spiritual messages. They sometimes charmed followers into giving up freedoms, jobs, former attachments, and money. Hare Krishnas were members of a U.S. Hindu movement. Clad in long robes,

Bodies of Jonestown members who took part in a **MASS SUICIDE** by drinking a cyanide-laced drink *(in foreground)* litter the ground in Guyana, South America.

they often danced and chanted with cymbals and drums in public places to attract new followers. The Unification Church was a religious movement that combined the teachings of its Korean founder, Sun Myung Moon, with Christian and Asian traditions. Moon became famous for the mass weddings he performed.

Jim Jones founded the Peoples Temple (Jonestown) in Indiana during the 1950s. He based the church on his version of moral and Communist beliefs. He advocated eliminating private property, owning goods in common, and strictly adhering to his rules as leader. The church moved to California in the 1960s, where it expanded. Almost from the beginning, reports of abuse and brainwashing leaked out. When the Internal Revenue Service and reporters investigated in 1977, Jones moved the church and his followers to Guyana, a South American country. The following year, California congressman Leo Ryan organized a delegation and traveled to Guyana to verify reports from families worried about their relatives. After a short and difficult visit, Ryan and his party—as well as several Jonestown residents who wished to leave the church—boarded two planes. But Jonestown loyalists and guards opened fire, killing Ryan and four others in his party. Then Jones and 912 followers lined up to drink a soft drink laced with poison in a mass suicide.

■ RELATIONSHIPS

Despite general disapproval, adults in the 1970s began speaking publicly about their nontraditional relationships and living arrangements. Transracial and homosexual relationships grew more visible. Some colleges started offering coed dorms. Single men and women lived together openly. "Marriages split and the birth rate dwindled as people took to publicly discussing modes of behavior that would have been unthinkable a few years earlier," observed author Loretta Britten.

Married couples still headed 71 percent of households. But between 1969 and 1975, divorces increased from 3 per 1,000 couples to 5.3 per 1,000 couples. Many states adopted no-fault divorce laws during this period. Such laws let couples divorce by mutual consent rather than assigning blame.

Heterosexual relationships had been changing since the introduction of birth control pills in 1960. The Pill freed women to use their bodies as they pleased. Some people labeled Pill users "loose." But millions of women took the Pill anyway, because it gave them freedom to plan their education and careers. In the 1970s, more women than ever attended college. Statistics showed women married later too. Many postponed or declined childbearing. A growing percentage of women chose careers over children. Most people still thought something was wrong with these women. But society was slowly beginning to understand that women should have choices for their future, as men did.

59

Male and female college students hang out in the hall at a **COED DORM** in 1970.

■ WOMEN'S LIBERATION

Earlier waves of the U.S. women's movement occurred in the late 1800s and early 1900s, as women fought for suffrage (voting rights). Another wave arose in the 1960s alongside other cries for civil rights. Both women and men protested war and inequalities of race and class. But women quickly tired of the discrimination they encountered in civil rights groups. Men raised in mainstream U.S. society took their superiority for granted. They expected women to serve as sidekicks, girlfriends, or secretaries. Women and men suffered the same beatings and arrests. Yet few organizations recognized women's contributions, a fact that emerged as one reason to revive the women's movement. "As a woman, an older woman, in a group of ministers who are accustomed to having women largely as supporters, there was no place for me to come into a leadership role," said prominent activist Ella Baker after volunteering for the Southern Christian Leadership Conference, a black civil rights group.

About the same time, Betty Friedan had caused a stir with her book *The Feminine Mystique*. Friedan's 1963 book asked women if they were truly satisfied with their lives. Her question struck a chord with women who felt constrained by gender roles. Her book helped refocus attention on the continuing need for women's equality.

During the 1960s, Congress had passed several civil rights laws designed to end job discrimination based on gender, race, religion, and nationality. But many employers ignored the laws. Few women were

Feminist and author **BETTY FRIEDAN** poses for a photo. On the table in front of her is her book *The Feminine Mystique*. The 1963 book inspired a generation of women to question traditional roles for women in society.

In an office setting, females typically worked as **SECRETARIES** *(above)*. Women in the 1970s started pursuing more fulfilling careers. And more pay too.

able to find jobs other than as teachers, nurses, maids, and secretaries. Those who did earned only fifty-nine cents for every dollar similarly qualified men made at the same jobs.

Although politicians spoke of women's career opportunities, they did little to change the employment landscape. H. R. Haldeman, Nixon's chief of staff, explained the lack of women in Nixon's administration: "The fact that we didn't have more [women] was a reflection of the time, and the nonvisibility of capable women: there weren't many female chairmen of banks, or of corporations, or religious leaders. There was a recognition of the need, but not a driving one."

Society still undervalued women. School history books failed to describe women's vital role in shaping society. In one 1972 textbook, only 5 of the 283 people mentioned were women. Language was another issue. Most writers used masculine pronouns (*he*, *his*, and so on) for both genders. This practice made females feel invisible. Many girls figured that such discussions didn't apply to them. Society called adult women either *Miss* or *Mrs.* These titles, unlike the male title *Mr.*, labeled women according to their marital status.

Women who wanted the same rights and opportunities as males called themselves feminists. In 1966 Friedan and other feminists had founded the

WOMEN MARCH FOR EQUALITY in New York City on August 26, 1970.

National Organization for Women (NOW). NOW vowed "to take action to bring American women into full participation in the mainstream of American society... in truly equal partnership with men." In 1970 NOW celebrated the fiftieth anniversary of woman suffrage with a national Women's Strike for Equality. Fifty thousand women marched in New York City with banners reading "Don't Iron While the Strike Is Hot" and "Don't Cook Dinner—Starve a Rat Today." Another one hundred thousand held rallies in forty-two states.

Throughout the 1970s, women assembled many groups and actions. Around the nation, women connected via rap (conversation) groups. They met in living rooms to discuss their status and help one another make changes. For example, women organized nationwide Take Back the Night vigils to protest sexual violence against women. The vigils became annual events on many college campuses after 1976. Feminists also actively lobbied for a wider role in society. The National Women's Political Caucus aimed to give women a stronger voice in politics. The First Women's Bank and Trust Company made it easier for women to get loans and credit independently.

The women's movement educated females about sex discrimination, which was common in U.S. homes, public life, and workplaces in the 1960s and 1970s. In 1962 fewer than one-third of women said they experienced discrimination. That portion doubled within a decade as women became more aware of sexism. Congress addressed this problem by passing the Equal Rights Amendment (ERA) to the Constitution in 1972. Suffragist Alice Paul had authored the ERA in 1923. It read: "Equality of rights under the law shall not be denied or abridged by the United States or any State on account of sex."

The bill moved to the state legislatures for ratification (approval). Women's groups around the country launched major rallies and petition drives. Within a year, thirty states had approved the amendment. Eight more states needed to ratify the amendment by 1979 for it to become law.

A backlash occurred instead. Organizations that supported traditional roles for women lobbied against the amendment. Outspoken conservative activist Phyllis Schlafly established a group called Stop ERA. Her group predicted outrageous results if ERA should pass. Schlafly supporters said ERA would result in unisex public bathrooms, pregnant women being drafted, and an end to child support and alimony. Some anti-ERA women attacked feminists personally. Hope Skillman Schary, two-term president of the National Council of Women of the United States, charged there was "no discrimination against women like they say there is and many of them [feminists] are just so unattractive. I wonder if they're completely well."

About 63 percent of Americans supported ERA. But Schlafly and her supporters pressured state legislators to vote against the bill. On October 6, 1978, Congress voted to extend the ratification deadline to June 1982. The extension didn't help. The bill fell three states short of the thirty-eight needed for ratification. But the battle for ERA continued to raise public awareness of women's rights.

63

Colleges and universities began recognizing women's contributions to society with special courses in women's studies. In 1974 about five hundred colleges offered two thousand courses in women's history, psychology, and sociology. Still, women's studies remained on the sidelines of education for at least another decade. And few elementary or high schools addressed gender imbalances in their curricula.

Language habits proved even slower to change. In 1972 the U.S. Government Printing Office approved the title *Ms.* for women who didn't want to be defined by their marital status. The same year, Gloria Steinem and members of the Women's Action Alliance founded *Ms.* magazine, which reinforced the term. But sexist language persisted in most publications and everyday usage.

Attitudes against married women working outside the home began to change during the 1970s. In 1936 a national survey had found that most men and women believed a woman shouldn't work if her husband did. In 1972 another study showed that the vast majority of men and women believed women could be wage earners too.

One of the most difficult fights feminists faced was for the legal right to a safe abortion. Ending pregnancy had always been a source of conflict. But outlawing abortion had never prevented it.

GLORIA STEINEM ON HOW WOMEN VOTE
MONEY FOR HOUSEWORK
NEW FEMINIST: SIMONE DE BEAUVOIR
BODY HAIR: THE LAST FRONTIER
WONDER WOMAN FOR PRESIDENT

The first issue of *MS. MAGAZINE* made a statement—not only with its bold cartoon art of Wonder Woman running for president but also with its editorial content.

Hundreds of women died each year because they couldn't find safe, legal abortions.

On March 3, 1970, attorneys Linda Coffee and Sarah Weddington challenged the ban on abortion in court. They represented a twenty-three-year-old pregnant ticket seller named Norma McCorvey, who had been raped and wanted to end her pregnancy. McCorvey lived in Texas, where state law prohibited abortion. To protect her privacy, McCorvey used the name Jane Roe in court. For the next two years, the case wound its way through different levels of courts. On October 11, 1972, Chief Justice Warren Burger decided the Supreme Court would make a final judgment.

Gloria Steinem has always been a journalist and feminist. But she never fit the wild and unattractive feminist stereotype shaped by conservatives. She was smart, beautiful, and soft-spoken.

Steinem started out as a reporter for *Esquire* magazine in 1962. She wrote an article that questioned women's place in society a year before publication of Friedan's book. The media noticed Steinem after she wrote about going undercover as a Playboy Club waitress. Steinem revealed how the Playboy company exploited, demeaned, and underpaid its female workers. Playboy Club waitresses wore high heels, skimpy costumes with cinched waists and stuffed breasts, and bunny tails customers liked to pull. The clubs had sprouted in many major U.S. cities after the success of *Playboy* men's magazine.

Publicizing Playboy policy cost Steinem dearly. She lost writing assignments with major general interest and traditional women's magazines. Playboy insiders harassed her repeatedly. Eventually the Playboy company sued her. But Steinem refused to shy away from controversy or be silenced.

In 1971 Steinem cofounded the Women's Action Alliance to bring together women's special interest groups. She led marches. She spoke nationwide with unusual wit and clarity to expose unfairness to women.

In 1972 Steinem helped launch *Ms.*

65

GLORIA STEINEM was a cofounder of *Ms.* magazine. She is a journalist and social activist who brought many feminist issues to the attention of the American public.

magazine. *Ms.* articles discussed serious women's issues, such as abuse and equal pay. They countered the pleasing-your-man articles typical of most women's magazines. Steinem also went on to write several books, including one that urged women to perform *Outrageous Acts and Everyday Rebellions* whenever possible.

As time passed, the media began to portray Steinem as a feminist leader. Critics of women's rights found—and still find—her a popular target.

On January 22, 1973, in a decision called *Roe v. Wade*, the Supreme Court established a woman's right to abortion based on her constitutional right to privacy. The decision also identified a fetus as "potential life," not a person. As such, the Court said, a fetus has no rights of its own. The decision limited abortion rights to the first two-thirds of pregnancy when a fetus cannot live outside the womb. The decision discouraged abortion in the last third of pregnancy, but said abortion must remain available throughout pregnancy to preserve a woman's health or to save her life. *Roe v. Wade* struck down antiabortion laws in thirty states. Antiabortion groups (mostly Christian conservatives) immediately began chipping away at the decision. But in the 1970s, women's health had won a huge victory.

■ IMMIGRATION ISSUES

Several other groups besides women faced social inequality in the 1970s. Among these were immigrants—both legal and illegal. Immigration patterns shifted during this decade. Newcomers from Asia and Latin America outnumbered Europeans and Canadians, the largest groups from previous generations. Like those before them, newcomers in the 1970s often experienced trouble adjusting and being accepted into U.S. society.

As U.S. troops withdrew from Southeast Asia in 1973, pro-U.S. residents started fleeing by the thousands. To help these Vietnamese, Cambodians, and Laotians, Congress raised the number of Southeast Asian refugees allowed into the country. Some urban areas welcomed the newcomers. But adjustment proved difficult. Americans spoke a language and followed customs few Southeast Asians understood. Local governments struggled to find teachers and doctors who could communicate with these immigrants. As their numbers swelled, some taxpayers grumbled about the cost of programs for foreigners unable to fit into U.S. culture.

The biggest anti-immigration uproar targeted Latin Americans coming from and through Mexico into California and Texas. Thousands of Mexicans each year risked their lives crossing the border for better-paying U.S. jobs. By 1970 about two hundred thousand Latino migrants per year were crossing U.S. borders illegally to find work.

The U.S. government had once welcomed Mexican laborers. The nation turned a blind eye to illegal immigrants because they performed low-wage, difficult but necessary tasks—such as manual farmwork—that many Americans wouldn't do. Lawmakers in the 1970s reacted differently. And legal farmworkers opposed the illegal immigrants, believing they stole jobs for lower wages. Some taxpayers demanded an end to free-flowing Latin American immigration. They believed these migrants, like Southeast Asians, used up limited U.S. resources.

To slow illegal immigration, the U.S. government increased border patrols. Border reinforcement largely failed. Instead, it led to more expensive and more dangerous crossings. Smugglers called coyotes charged higher fees and took more risks to lead illegal migrants across deserts, mountains, and back roads. Many immigrants died in the desert and in secret compartments of vehicles. Employers who hired only from coyotes took advantage of the workers' illegal status and inability to speak English. They paid very low wages, offered terrible work and living conditions, and treated workers poorly.

The rise in illegal immigration attracted more legal farmworkers to unions, such as the United Farm Workers. Union workers banded together to negotiate with bosses. As a result, legal workers saw small improvements in pay, hours, treatment on the job, and living conditions. But no one spoke for illegal immigrants. Their status and daily lives remained dismal.

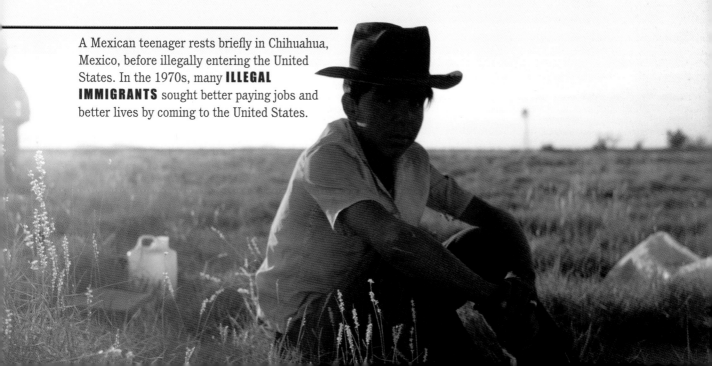

A Mexican teenager rests briefly in Chihuahua, Mexico, before illegally entering the United States. In the 1970s, many **ILLEGAL IMMIGRANTS** sought better paying jobs and better lives by coming to the United States.

■ BLACK PROGRESS, PRIDE, AND LINGERING PREJUDICE

The African American population in the 1970s had increased 37 percent over the 1960s. According to the 1970 U.S. census, blacks totaled about 11 percent of the population. Their numbers grew especially fast in cities.

At the same time, the number of urban whites decreased by 13 percent. As communities integrated (became racially mixed), some whites feared being outnumbered by blacks. Many white families fled to suburbs and to southern states.

Whites who moved because of race issues blamed their migration on school busing policies. In 1954 the Supreme Court had outlawed separate schools for black and white children in a decision called *Brown v. Board of Education*. Segregated southern districts largely ignored the ruling. In 1971 the court revisited the issue and affirmed that busing would help schools achieve racial balance and better education for all students. This decision unleashed a string of protests in all-white urban areas. Some white parents believed racial mixing in classrooms would damage their children's education.

President Nixon halted busing until Congress could create laws to guide busing plans. A 1973 education bill let districts appeal court-ordered busing, which delayed the start of many busing programs. This bill never considered the benefits of educating black and white students together. In 1974 President Ford established busing boundaries. Later court decisions by various federal and local courts limited the time children spent on the bus. These rulings appeased families who valued neighborhood schools for their children.

Rulings were mixed over the next decade. In 1974 a judge's order increased the number of bused students from 14,900 to 25,000 in the white neighborhood of South Boston, Massachusetts. This order triggered violent protests. Within two years, parents removed 17,216 white students from Boston public schools and

In 1974 a judge's order increased the number of bused students from 14,900 to 25,000 in the white neighborhood of South Boston, Massachusetts.

Police motorcycles escort a group of **SCHOOL BUSES CARRYING AFRICAN AMERICAN STUDENTS** through the streets of South Boston, Massachusetts. A court decision resulted in a higher ratio of black to white students in Boston's city schools.

enrolled them in suburban or private schools. Meanwhile, the Michigan Supreme Court dismissed a plan to bus the city's black children to white suburban schools. Other courts approved busing plans for Denver, Colorado; Louisville, Kentucky; and Columbus, Ohio.

Another explosive issue involved the use of affirmative action to improve opportunities for blacks. Proponents of affirmative action wanted businesses and schools to reserve places for minorities. The idea was to right centuries of wrongs that had kept blacks out of higher education and in low-level positions.

In 1971 the Supreme Court agreed in *Griggs v. Duke Power Company* that race cannot be a reason to segregate workers. Duke required all employees who requested promotions from the lowest-paying manual labor departments to have a high school diploma or pass an intelligence test. But given the local education system and lack of community advantages, the Court considered both criteria biased toward whites. The justices ordered Duke to create a test that gave blacks and whites equal chances at passing. After this ruling, employers had to consider minority experiences and carefully avoid indirect or unintentional discrimination.

The U.S. Department of Labor used the ruling to force antiblack unions nationwide to admit minorities. Soon jobs as police officers, firefighters, and construction workers opened to blacks and Latinos. Union leaders and employers realized that meeting affirmative action goals ensured against being sued for discrimination.

Like any social change, affirmative action attracted critics. Some qualified whites believed they'd lost jobs to less qualified minority applicants because companies had racial hiring quotas (that designated a certain number of jobs for minorities). For example, white student Allan Bakke had applied to the University of California–Davis medical school and was rejected. Bakke, a Vietnam vet and NASA engineer, claimed that he'd scored higher on entrance exams than sixteen accepted minority students. He sued the school, charging discrimination. The 1978 Supreme Court decision waffled. In a 5–4 decision, judges ordered the school to enroll Bakke and outlawed university quotas for minority students. But the Court also said universities could consider race as one factor in admissions.

Not much changed in the public mind. Some whites believed quotas were unjust. Many blacks believed quotas were still necessary to improve education and career opportunities for their children.

Despite these conflicts, African Americans made considerable social and political progress. College enrollment of black students jumped from 282,000 in 1966 to 1,062,000 in 1976.

ALLAN BAKKE attends school at the University of California–Davis. The Supreme Court found that the university had unfairly rejected Bakke's application due to reverse racial discrimination.

ALEX HALEY *(left)* wrote the popular novel *Roots* based on his own African and African American ancestry. Activist **ANGELA DAVIS** *(right)* speaks to a crowd in 1974.

Black entertainers gained lead parts in movies and television shows. Black authors won high honors. Between 1960 and 1970, the number of black congresspeople had risen to fifteen. By 1972 eighty-six black mayors ran cities, such as Cleveland, Ohio; Gary, Indiana; and Washington D.C. In Illinois, Michigan, New York, and California, black politicians became powerful enough to organize committees that could handle problems specific to their communities.

Black pride swelled after Alex Haley's book *Roots* appeared in 1976. The novel traced Haley's ancestry back to an eighteenth-century African slave. This book, as well as the 1977 TV miniseries by the same name, showcased the black experience in the United States and inspired pride in African heritage. Proud blacks began calling themselves "African American." Meanwhile, many whites were still trying to get used to saying "black" instead of "Negro," a term that blacks no longer found acceptable.

Black progress and pride only inflamed the hatred of some whites. J. Edgar Hoover, director of the FBI, ordered his detectives to dog groups advocating black power. He feared they wanted to overthrow the government. Hoover ordered spying on big-name leaders, such as scholar and activist Angela Davis; author Eldridge Cleaver; Jesse Jackson, founder of Operation PUSH (People United to Serve Humanity); and Black Panther Party founder Bobby Seale.

Other blacks in the limelight received their share of prejudice too. In 1973, for example, African American baseball player Hank Aaron approached Babe Ruth's 1927 home run record. He received about three thousand letters per day. Sadly, most came from racists threatening Aaron's life.

■ NATIVE AMERICANS

Native Americans carried out a struggle for equality similar to that of African Americans. In November 1969, about one hundred American Indians had occupied the abandoned Alcatraz Island near San Francisco. Alcatraz had once been a famous prison, and before that it was Native American land.

The activists were a mix of students, tribal leaders, and members of a new organization called the American Indian Movement (AIM). They stayed until June 1971, calling attention to centuries of injustice and disrespect toward Native Americans. AIM's long-range goal was to restore pride among the hundreds of American Indian nations and reverse the damage done to them by the U.S. government's economic, political, and social neglect and corruption.

The Alcatraz takeover instilled new self-confidence in many Native Americans and raised their visibility. Building on this success, AIM launched a series of protests against civil rights abuses Indians experienced. One high-profile protest began on February 27, 1973. About three hundred Native Americans occupied the village at Wounded Knee, South Dakota. (In 1890 the U.S. Army had massacred

In 1973 members of the Oglala Sioux march to the cemetery in **WOUNDED KNEE,** South Dakota, where their ancestors were buried after the 1890 massacre there.

more than two hundred unarmed Sioux there. Historians consider that conflict the final major battle between Native Americans and federal soldiers.) About fifty-six hundred Native Americans came and went over the course of the occupation. Some brought their families. After seventy-one days, the U.S. military forced the Native Americans to leave. During the incident, two people died, twelve were wounded, and almost twelve hundred people were arrested.

The government tried to prosecute AIM members for the takeover. But judges dismissed the court case for lack of evidence. The FBI continued to harass AIM leaders throughout the decade by arresting or suing them on trumped-up charges. Although Alcatraz inspired few changes, the occupation called attention to the government's poor handling of Native American affairs.

AIM organized dozens of protests during the 1970s. The group's last major event of the decade was the Longest Walk of 1978. Several hundred people marched peacefully from San Francisco to Washington, D.C., to symbolize the forced removal of American Indians from their homelands. Their walk highlighted the growing congressional backlash against treaty rights and created considerable media buzz.

The Red Power movement (the organized effort to promote Native American rights) remained strong until the late 1970s. Attention stirred by the movement resulted in federal support for Native American self-rule. Funding increased for American Indian healthcare, education, housing, and substance abuse programs.

■ DISABILITY RIGHTS

Americans with disabilities faced social barriers similar to those faced by ethnic and racial minorities. Mainstream society considered people with handicaps mentally or physically unfit to participate in community life, recreation programs, and work. Physical obstacles often prevented people with physical disabilities from gaining access to such activities too. To make matters worse, a variety of state laws blocked people with disabilities from voting, marrying, having children, being seen in public, or attending public school. Too many children and adults with disabilities were trapped in institutions.

Americans with disabilities wanted to speak for themselves and choose where and how they would live. They noted research that showed

73

racial integration improved education. Activists figured this research applied to students with disabilities as well. People with disabilities might need adapted school, work, and home environments. But the adaptations were worth the potential benefits to all U.S. society.

Like other 1970s activists, disabiity groups took their message into the streets. Poster-carrying wheelchair users and able-bodied people sympathetic to their cause marched, organized boycotts, and blocked traffic to gain attention. Congress responded with the Rehabilitation Act of 1973. Section 504 of the act guaranteed fair access to federally funded programs. The law stated that government could withhold funds from any educational or vocational program, health-care or human services setting, or place of employment that blocked opportunities solely because of disability. This law was the first national public statement against disability discrimination.

Two years later, Congress passed the Education for All Handicapped Children Act. This law required public school districts to provide free, appropriate education to everyone ages three to twenty-one years. It further required that education be in the least restrictive environment. This phrase ensured that students with disabilities would learn alongside nondisabled students whenever they could benefit from the setting.

President Ford's advisers drafted laws to support these acts. But the Carter administration dragged its heels. Disability activists tired of waiting for the new federal regulations. Early in 1977, they organized nationwide protests. In one bold move, 150 protesters occupied the San Francisco offices of the federal Department of Health, Education, and Welfare for twenty-six days.

On April 28, the federal government published guidelines for architectural changes and other requirements for making facilities and programs accessible to people with disabilities. Many employers, civil servants, and administrators opposed the new laws because local schools, businesses, and governments had to pay for the changes. For decades to come, people with disabilities fought in courts to gain entry to mainstream programs and buildings.

The requirement for least restrictive environments led to emptying of institutions by the end of the decade. Change came slowly in some regions. But people with disabilities gradually found more opportunities to live, work, and learn with their able-bodied neighbors.

■ GAY AND LESBIAN RIGHTS

In the early 1970s, many state laws prohibited consenting adults from having same-sex partners. Some laws punished gays and lesbians with jail sentences of up to twenty years. In Michigan anyone caught repeating the offense could receive life imprisonment. Some religious leaders preached that homosexuality was a sin rather than an inborn orientation. Negative public opinion and harsh laws often led to police harassment and hate crimes.

As a result, most gays kept their sexual orientation hidden, or "in the closet." Those who "came out," or publicly acknowledged their sexual preference, were often fired, avoided, or ousted from work and other groups. Author Rita Mae Brown wrote that one of her friends coped with being gay in a hostile world by acting "straight as a stick at work and gay as soon as he left it."

On June 28, 1969, police raided the Stonewall Inn, a gay bar on Christopher Street in New York City, and ordered its customers to leave. A large, angry group gathered outside. "Hundreds of young men went on a rampage," wrote the *New York Times*. "The young men threw bricks, bottles, garbage, pennies, and a parking meter at the policemen. . . ." When the riot ended, four police were hurt and thirteen rioters

Young people gathered in front of the **STONEWALL INN** the weekend after police riots wreaked havoc in the New York neighborhood. The 1969 riots are an important event in the history of gay and lesbian rights.

were arrested. The event sparked riots for a week afterward. Ever larger crowds returned to Christopher Street to protest treatment of homosexuals. Hundreds of supporters shouted, "We want freedom!" and "Gay power!"

The Stonewall riots triggered a gay pride movement in New York. Similar movements sprang up in Los Angeles, San Francisco, and Chicago. In 1970 these groups celebrated the anniversary of the Stonewall riots by marching in their cities. The parade became an annual event in major cities across the nation. By 1973 the number of gay and lesbian organizations climbed to eight hundred. Gays and lesbians in big cities began to feel more comfortable acknowledging publicly that they were homosexual.

Gays and lesbians continued making headlines and gaining small successes. In 1973 the American Psychiatric Association declared that homosexuality was not a mental disorder. Cities and states added the phrase *sexual preference* to antidiscrimination laws. In 1975 the Civil Service Commission reversed its ban on hiring homosexuals for most federal jobs. Some religions, such as Unitarians and Reformed Jews, allowed gay and lesbian ministers and rabbis.

In 1977, when Harvey Milk won a seat on the San Francisco Board of Supervisors (city council), he became the first openly gay elected official of any large U.S. city. Milk represented San Francisco's Castro neighborhood, where most residents were gay or lesbian. Milk encouraged gay pride and worked hard to enact a gay rights law. The only vote against the law came from Dan White, a conservative supervisor. White quit the board in protest soon thereafter. But White changed his mind and requested reappointment from Mayor George Moscone. Milk advised Moscone to reject White's request.

On November 27, 1978, White slipped into city hall and fatally shot Moscone and Milk. That night about twenty-five thousand gay and straight San Franciscans mourned their dead leaders with a spontaneous and peaceful candlelight march from the Castro neighborhood to city hall.

HARVEY MILK *(left)* and Mayor George Moscone *(right)* attend the signing of San Francisco's gay rights bill in 1977.

White turned himself in and stood trial for murder. Though evidence clearly showed that he'd planned the killings, he claimed he hadn't. His excuse was depression made worse by eating lots of junk food. His argument became known as the Twinkie defense. White got off with a light sentence of seven years and eight months in jail. (He committed suicide shortly after his release.)

Conservative media portrayed White as a protector of eroding U.S. values. Most fair-minded people, however, were angry about his sentence. After hearing about the sentence, four thousand men and women gathered at city hall and vented their anger in a riot. Some enraged mourners torched police cars, smashed windows, and disabled buses. A few hours later, dozens of police officers attacked a bar in the Castro neighborhood. The two riots became known as the White Night riots.

Even in death, Milk's voice continued to encourage the gay pride movement. "If a bullet should enter my brain," he tape-recorded in his will, "let that bullet destroy every closet door." He called on gays in every walk of life to "come out, stand up and let the world know. Only that way will we start to achieve our rights."

In 1971 editors in the newsroom at the *New York Times* discuss a court order to temporarily halt publication of the Pentagon Papers. This series was critical of U.S. policy in Vietnam. In the 1970s, NEWSPAPERS were the primary news media for most Americans.

CHAPTER SIX

WRITE ON:
PRINT MEDIA IN THE 1970s

During the 1970s, reporters and authors broached subjects few writers had tackled before. They explored new aspects of old topics. Writers interpreted these subjects for the decade's three main print media: newspapers, magazines, and books.

■ NEWSPAPERS

Before widespread television viewing, most major cities published both morning and afternoon newspapers to serve the rush-hour crowds in urban areas. By the 1970s, many readers were skipping the afternoon paper and watching evening news on television instead. But in 1971, sixty-six cities still produced two or more daily newspapers—at least one morning and one afternoon edition. Each was filled with advertisements that earned newspaper companies most of their money. Weekend papers included sections for comics, world news, home and garden, business, real estate, and separate information geared toward women.

Because newspapers were so popular in the 1970s, journalists exerted extraordinary influence on public opinion and policy. Newspapers first published the damning Pentagon Papers. Investigative reporters exposed crimes that led to President Nixon's downfall. In response to the *New York Times* Pentagon Papers publication, White House chief of staff,

79

> " To the ordinary guy, all this is a bunch of gobbledygook. But out of the gobbledygook comes a very clear thing: You can't trust the government; you can't believe what they say; and you can't rely on their judgment. "

—H. R. Haldeman, June 14, 1971,

reacting to the *New York Times* publication of the Pentagon Papers

H. R. Haldeman, told Nixon: "To the ordinary guy, all this is a bunch of gobbledygook. But out of the gobbledygook comes a very clear thing: You can't trust the government; you can't believe what they say; and you can't rely on their judgment. And the implicit infallibility [accepted wisdom] of presidents, which has been an accepted thing in America, is badly hurt by this, because it shows that people do things the President wants to do even though it's wrong, and the President can be wrong."

Newspaper owners became very powerful. Owners of large chains wielded the greatest power. They could slant the news for readers across the nation. For example, the Hearst family controlled the content of newspapers in more than fifteen cities in the 1970s.

■ MAGAZINES

Changing popular culture and a poor economy hurt longtime magazines in the 1970s. *Life* had begun in 1936 as the first weekly U.S. photojournalism magazine. Its main competitor, the biweekly *Look*, launched one year later. Both magazines remained very popular for three decades, and *Life* won many awards. But as TV cut into magazines' ad income and postal rates rose, *Look* and *Life* found turning a profit difficult. The magazines folded in 1971 and 1972, respectively. *Life* revived later in the decade as a monthly.

The decade's most popular journals focused on limited subjects and targeted specific populations. *People* magazine gave starstruck Americans gossip articles and photos of their favorite entertainers. *Sports Illustrated* had begun in 1954 as a resource covering elite sports, such as yachting and polo. By the 1970s, the magazine appealed to the public's growing interest in exercise. The magazine expanded to cover sports the general population followed, such as football, tennis, swimming, and baseball.

The Hearst family had been media giants for decades. They owned many newspapers and magazines. As one of the wealthiest and most influential families in the United States, they were perfect targets for antiestablishment groups.

One such group, the Symbionese Liberation Army (SLA), wanted money and attention for their cause. They also wanted a hostage to swap for two imprisoned SLA members. SLA members kidnapped nineteen-year-old Patty Hearst from her Berkeley apartment on February 4, 1974. She had been living there with her fiancé while attending the University of California.

The SLA sent tapes to Patty's father, Randolph Hearst, ordering him to give San Francisco's poor six million dollars in food to save Patty's life. This demand came after Hearst refused any part in a prisoner swap. Three months after the kidnapping, another tape arrived from the SLA. On this recording, Patty said she had joined the SLA. She declared her family "the pig Hearsts."

A stunned nation followed the story in newspapers and on television. Meanwhile, police conducted a major hunt for the heiress. In April Patty resurfaced in a bank robbery with her captors. A bank videotape showed her wearing an SLA beret and toting a gun.

A bank security camera views PATTY HEARST, daughter of wealthy newspaper mogul Randolph Hearst, during a 1974 SLA robbery.

81

Patty and two others hid for sixteen months before being caught. At her trial, Patty said her kidnappers had drugged and threatened to kill her. Then they brainwashed her. The jury refused to believe her. They gave her a seven-year sentence for gun possession and robbery. In 1979 President Carter shortened Patty's sentence, and she went free after twenty-one months. She married her former bodyguard and published an autobiography titled *Every Secret Thing* in 1982. President Bill Clinton pardoned her in 2001.

JOHN H. JOHNSON, publisher of *Ebony* and *Ebony Jr!*, sits at his desk in Chicago, Illinois. Johnson later became the first African American to appear on *Forbes* magazine's list of the four hundred wealthiest Americans.

For the new generation of feminists who craved serious reading, *Ms.* magazine offered information about equal pay for equal work, laws against physical and emotional abuse, and the right to safe health care. *Ms.* offered a more independent view of womanhood than did other women's magazines, such as the long-running and still popular *Good Housekeeping*, *Redbook*, and *Cosmopolitan*.

Cosmopolitan was the first homemaker-oriented magazine to get a 1970s makeover. Editor in chief Helen Gurley Brown embraced the sexual revolution. She modernized the magazine with covers of women in revealing clothes. She published the first women's magazine article about sex outside marriage. Her most shocking issue featured a nude centerfold of actor Burt Reynolds.

Children in the 1970s chose from both new and old magazines. *Highlights for Children*, launched in 1946, was still going strong. *Kids*, a magazine created and edited by children with little adult input, was published from 1970 to 1974. *Ebony Jr!*, an offshoot of the adult *Ebony* magazine, began in 1973. Both *Ebony* journals featured black history and culture. *Cricket*, a literary magazine for children, was born in 1973 and eventually grew into a large family of popular children's magazines.

■ BOOKS

Authors of the 1970s wrote books about a range of topics, from entertaining to serious. Light fiction by Harold Robbins, John le Carré, and Judith Krantz topped adult best-seller lists. Novels by established authors Irving Wallace, Leon Uris, and John Updike continued to sell well.

Harlequin romance novels debuted in the United States during the 1970s. Their Canadian publisher contracted to distribute its popular line through the U.S. company Pocket Books. Harlequin aimed the short, inexpensive paperbacks at female readers, and women loved them. Harlequin authors cranked out scores of fast reads with steamy plots that suggested sex rather than describing specific acts.

Horror books became a popular genre in the mid-1970s thanks to Stephen King. King wrote long, creepy character studies that flew off bookstore shelves. His first novel, *Carrie*, became a best-seller in 1974 and a movie in 1976. Critics often hailed King as the king of horror.

If King had a queen, it was Joyce Carol Oates. Her first novel, *With Shuddering Fall*, was published in 1964. Oates's novels, like King's, showcased suspense, violence, and misfit characters. During the 1970s, she published such bone chillers as *Wonderland* (1971), *The Assassins* (1975), and *Son of the Morning* (1978). "Horror is a fact of life," Oates told one reporter, "and as a writer I'm fascinated with all facets of life."

STEPHEN KING is an author of creepy horror stories. Many of them have been turned into movies.

Science fiction, long a popular and serious genre, turned lighthearted and thoughtful with Kurt Vonnegut (1922–2007). His quirky stories questioned the United States' growing materialism. Vonnegut's writing drew from his experiences with war and death. He used the irony of personal tragedies as springboards for *Happy Birthday, Wanda June* (1971), *Breakfast of Champions* (1973), and *Slapstick* (1976).

Meanwhile, new voices emerged and challenged readers to think about life differently. White males no longer attracted most of publishers' and critics' attention. Female, black, and Latino authors, such as Mexican American poet Ana Castillo, gained broader audiences.

Racism, an important subject in the 1960s, continued to play a role in 1970s literature. Ernest Gaines's *The Autobiography of Miss Jane Pittman* (1971) studied slavery across generations through the eyes of one woman. Five years later, Alex Haley published *Roots: The Saga of an American Family*. Alice Walker had written many articles, short stories, and poems before her first book, *The Third Life of Grange Copeland*, a disguised autobiography, appeared in 1970. She focused on the civil rights movement in her second novel, *Meridian* (1976).

ALICE WALKER'S first book was published in 1970. She went on to become the first African American woman to receive a Pulitzer Prize for Fiction for her novel *The Color Purple* (1983).

Children's literature entered a reality phase in the 1970s. Characters died. Parents divorced. Readers learned that life could be grim, even for a child. And they learned to question authority, as their baby boomer parents had done.

Even humorous fiction tackled serious topics. Young-adult author Judy Blume dared to write about menstruation, the value of religion, and selecting the perfect first bra in *Are You There God? It's Me, Margaret* (1970). The same year, she published *Iggie's House* about racism. She took on divorce in *It's Not the End of the World* (1972) and bullies in *Blubber* (1974). In one of her more daring books, *Forever* (1975), Blume explored teenage sexuality.

Blume's books struck a chord with readers. But adults who wanted to keep these issues from their kids felt outrage. Many sought to ban her books from schools and public libraries. One angry parent called Blume a Communist after reading *Are You There God? It's Me, Margaret*. "I never did

JUDY BLUME became a controversial figure for her books, which tackled sensitive subjects such as teenage sexuality.

figure out if she equated Communism with menstruation or religion, the two major concerns in twelve-year-old Margaret's life," Blume wrote on her website. The author's many critics inspired her to launch a campaign against book banning that continues in the twenty-first century.

85

Toni Morrison rose to fame in the 1970s. Her novels examined the experiences of black men and women in a racist society. Her first book, *The Bluest Eye* (1970), established her as a powerful character writer. In 1973 *Sula* earned Morrison the National Book Critics Circle Award. And her thought-provoking *Song of Solomon* (1977) became the first book by an African American author chosen since 1949 for the Book of the Month Club (a mail-order bookseller).

Feminist artist Judy Chicago created *THE DINNER PARTY*
(1974–1979). Thirty-nine place settings, each commemorating
an important woman from history, surround a triangular table.

CHAPTER SEVEN

EXPERIMENTS IN CREATIVITY:

ART, DESIGN, AND FASHION IN THE 1970s

For visual artists of all kinds, the 1970s provided a time to refine the modern styles introduced in the 1960s. Many artists conveyed messages through color, format, and fashion. Both men and women discovered unusual ways to express their creativity through light, shape, and media.

■ WOMEN ARTISTS GAIN ACCEPTANCE

87

Women had participated in every art movement since the beginning of time. But few gained recognition for their talents. Before the 1970s, most art galleries and museums had refused to exhibit female artists. Their work took second place to men's regardless of its quality. The women's movement pried open the art world's closed doors.

Women's art in the 1970s tended to emphasize the female body, women's history, and female spirituality. Feminists elevated decorative arts and crafts once dismissed as housework—such as quilting, sewing, and pottery—to high art. Women protested the injustices they suffered through these and other art forms. May Stevens's 1970 painting *Big Daddy Paper Doll* (1970) dealt with male authority. Faith Ringgold's prison mural *For the Woman's House* (1971) offered a tribute to women in all walks of life. Nancy Spero's 1974 painting *Torture in Chile* (1974) exposed government torture in South America.

Faith Ringgold created *FOR THE WOMAN'S HOUSE* in 1971. In this piece, she portrays women from different ethnic backgrounds in various roles, from bus driver to professional sports player to doctor.

Some women artists placed females in settings previously reserved for men. Mary Beth Edelson's *Some Living American Women Artists/Last Supper* (1971) replaced the thirteen men in a biblical Last Supper scene with likenesses of female artists. Edelson painted artist Georgia O'Keeffe as a female Jesus and other artists, such as Helen Frankenthaler, Lee Krasner, and Louise Nevelson, as apostles (followers). Edelson wanted to "bring women artists, for the first time, to the table of history." Judy Chicago also used the Last Supper theme for her mixed-media work *The Dinner Party*.

Graphic designers transferred images of female protest and pride onto T-shirts, buttons, postcards, and murals. Portraits of women heroes included Vietnamese women soldiers and American black activist Angela Davis. Graphic artist Yolanda Lopez explained, "[T]hought and image came together in this era."

■ INSTALLATION ART

The 1970s saw an increase in installation art. Installation art uses sculptural materials and other media to change the way people experience a particular space. Installation artists often create large scenes with objects that symbolize a story or concept.

During the 1970s, some artists added video images to their installations. These videos often showed one part of the body or someone performing an activity. Video art forced observers to linger. But it was difficult to move, hang over a sofa at home, or show without electronic equipment. Like other types of installation art, video art works best in a large public environment, such as a museum.

Judy Cohen was born on July 20, 1939, in Chicago, Illinois. At a young age, she dreamed of becoming an artist. She began taking classes at the Art Institute of Chicago in 1945. To complete her studies, she went to the University of California–Los Angeles (UCLA). As a fervent feminist, she stayed in California to form the first women's art program at California State University in Fresno. In 1970 Judy changed her last name to Chicago "to liberate herself from male-dominated stereotypes" that people might associate with Cohen, a common Jewish surname.

In 1974 Chicago focused on women's history in her art. When Chicago created *The Dinner Party*, she honored more than one thousand women. The work was a triangular banquet table measuring 48 feet (15 meters) per side set for thirty-nine "women of achievement" from "various stages of Western civilization."

Chicago and her team of artists painted and molded symbols representing these women on oversize china plates. Many plates featured sculptures that looked like butterflies or flowers and symbolized the female vulva. The plates sat on runners embroidered with each woman's story. The table stood on porcelain floor tiles inscribed with 999 women's names. "This would suggest that the women at the table had risen from a foundation provided by other women's accomplishments, and each plate

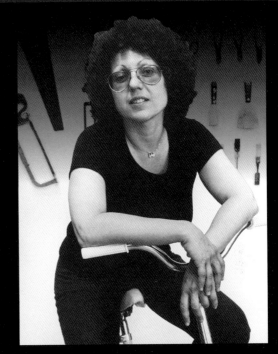

JUDY CHICAGO'S *Dinner Party* is on permanent display at the Brooklyn Museum in New York.

89

would then symbolize not only a particular woman but also the tradition from which she emerged," Chicago explained.

The Dinner Party took hundreds of volunteers from 1974 until 1979 to complete. Once finished, several major museums rejected it because it was art by women and about women. But smaller venues welcomed the installation, and *The Dinner Party* made a national tour. At each stop, the art provoked excitement and controversy. In the end, Chicago and her display raised awareness of women in art, history, and other aspects of Western culture.

During the 1970s, many local governments realized that public art could improve a city's image. Several cities, such as Chicago, San Francisco, and Salt Lake City, began commissioning street art for the enjoyment of citizens passing by.

Chicago led the way. In 1974 sculptor and painter Marc Chagall presented Chicago with his gift of a huge four-sided mosaic called *The Four Seasons*. In the same year, metal sculptor Alexander Calder dedicated his shocking red, 35-ton (32-metric ton) steel sculpture *Flamingo*. "The Loop [downtown Chicago] is now one of the world's largest outdoor museums for contemporary art," said Chicago's mayor, Richard J. Daley.

Later in 1974, the city passed a law requiring any new public building to leave space for artwork. The Chicago Public Art Program, which sprang from this law, ensured the tradition would continue. Since then Chicago's courthouses, libraries, and police stations have displayed more than four hundred pieces of art.

PUBLIC ART SCULPTURE *Flamingo* by Alexander Calder stands in downtown Chicago, Illinois.

By the end of the decade, performance artists joined video artists in challenging the idea that art must be stationary. Many performance artists took their live shows into the streets. They exhibited before crowds in restaurants, malls, and parks. They sought audience reactions or emphasized particular points of view.

■ARCHITECTURE

Modern architects Louis Kahn, Frank Gehry, and I. M. Pei completed some of their most famous buildings in the 1970s. Kahn's Phillips Exeter Academy Library in Exeter, New Hampshire (1972), received an American Institute of Architects (AIA) award. Gehry jump-started his career with the design of his own house in Santa Monica, California (1978). In the same year, Pei finished the Dallas City Hall, a seven-story inverted prism in Texas.

Skyscrapers made big news in the 1970s. In 1972 New York City's World Trade Center towers became the world's tallest buildings. They snatched the record from New York's Empire State Building, which had held it for forty-one years. Then, in 1973, the architectural firm of Skidmore, Owings and Merrill completed the 110-story Sears Tower in downtown Chicago. The bronze-tinted structure stood as the world's tallest building for twenty-three years.

Throughout the 1970s, urban architects experimented with glass and steel and tried to conserve resources with their designs. In 1977 Hugh Stubbins

FRANK GEHRY'S home *(below)* in Santa Monica, California, is constructed of a light wood frame, corrugated metal, and chain link fencing.

revolutionized skyscraper heating. He included solar panels in his design for New York City's Citicorp Center. The main tower soared above an unusual plaza containing four massive support columns.

■ FAR OUT, FUNKY FASHIONS

Fashion in the 1970s was a free-for-all. Clothes and hairstyles often turned into political statements. Trendy folks copied the styles of television stars. Others worked so hard to rebel against high fashion that they created a uniform of their own.

For the first time in decades, men's fashions offered choices in colors and styles. Pastel shirts peeked out of wide-lapel three-piece suits. Business and formal attire included shirts with cuffs and cuff links. Shirts sported button-down collars or collars with stays (plastic strips) inside to keep them looking crisp. Wide, brightly colored ties came in floral patterns or splashy designs. Polyester was a popular fabric for bell-bottom pants and leisure suits. A leisure suit consisted of a shirtlike jacket and matching pants. These suits came in many

FUNKY FASHIONS were a way for people of the 1970s to express their individuality. Miniskirts, shorts known as hotpants, and bell bottom jeans were popular fashion in the 1970s.

colors and patterns and often appeared with patterned shirts and platform shoes.

Women of the 1970s wore everything from miniskirts and hot pants (very short shorts) to midiskirts and maxiskirts (calf- and ankle-length skirts). Early in the decade, women's clothes fit more loosely, and layering was popular. Sweaters or vests covered shirts that drooped over long, full skirts. Because clothes were loose and layered, many women shed their bras. Others wore newfangled bras made from soft fabrics that followed the body's natural shape.

High boots finished the look. Boots and shoes usually had thick soles. Wood-soled exercise sandals and clogs were especially popular. Manufacturers began to make women's shoes rounded in front for easier walking and running.

The baggy look got a boost from the movie *Annie Hall* in 1977. The title character's mismatched mannish outfits included oversize layered shirts, polka-dot neckties, vests and jackets, baggy chino pants, and a bowler hat.

Disco fashions attracted a large following toward the end of the decade. The 1977 movie *Saturday Night Fever* helped popularize disco music, dancing, and clothing. One appeal of disco fashion was a growing backlash against looser styles of the 1960s and early 1970s. Women dancers preferred feminine styles with slinky spaghetti-strapped dresses, satin boxer shorts, leotards, and glow-in-the-dark makeup and nail polish.

■ JEANS AND T-SHIRTS

Denim trousers had been around for centuries as work pants for sailors, farmers, and laborers. In the 1950s, rebellious youths began wearing jeans as everyday

JOHN TRAVOLTA strikes a disco pose in *Saturday Night Fever*. The 1977 movie and the dance style inspired a new clothing fad.

> ## "To wear plain jeans and dark colors was to reject the more-is-better, new-is-better mentality."

—Beverly Gordon, 1991, describing counterculture fashion of the 1960s and 1970s

attire. By the 1960s, jeans had become a political statement against conformity. Author Beverly Gordon observed, "To wear plain jeans and dark colors was to reject the more-is-better, new-is-better mentality."

Blue denim developed into a symbol of the baby boomer generation. Manufacturers turned denim into jackets, shorts, skirts, and upholstery. In 1974 American Motors Corporation even upholstered some car models with denim.

To personalize their jeans, people decorated them with beads, sequins, bells, and embroidery. Punk stylists added velvet, leopard print, and plastic.

Professional clothing designers spotted a business opportunity. They began producing upscale, brand-name jeans that claimed to help wearers look unique. But unusual jeans cost unusually high prices. A few companies still manufactured ordinary jeans. But by the end of the 1970s, more than thirty companies created designer jeans with trendy labels on the pockets, legs, or waistbands. Calvin Klein and Ralph Lauren established their designer kingdoms with jeans. The era of trendy jeans at outrageous prices was born.

Fancy, formfitting T-shirts—rather than boxy, 1960s tie-dyes—topped the new high-end jeans. The snug cap-sleeve shirts for women often carried personalized messages, embroidery, or pictures. Political statements, jokes, and pictures of celebrities adorned simple cotton shirts for men. All were meant to make a statement about the wearer.

■ GROOVY HAIRSTYLES

In the 1970s, hairstyles varied as much as fashion. Natural, no-fuss hair fit hippie lifestyles, and big hair suited trendy types. Many men waited longer between barber visits—if they went at all—and their sideburns grew to the bottoms of their ears.

People chose Afros (tight curls cut in a full, evenly rounded shape), dreadlocks (matted, twisted locks of hair), or cornrows (rows of hair tightly braided close to the scalp) to show their ethnic pride—or simply because they liked the look. People of all races wore Afros. Jamaican reggae singer Bob Marley introduced Americans to dreadlocks. Cornrows, which had originated long ago in Africa, grew popular alongside black pride. In the 1979 movie *10*, Bo Derek gave millions of white people permission to wear cornrows.

Free-flowing curls were popular for males and females. Some women piled them on top of their heads for a retro look. Those without natural curls crimped or permed their hair. Layered haircuts helped give a curly look to straight-haired folks. Farrah Fawcett-Majors, star of the popular television show *Charlie's Angels*, inspired many girls and women to layer their long hair into flowing, off-the-shoulder waves. Some topped their curly heads with scarves, skullcaps, or turbans.

Millions of American women and girls styled their hair after **FARRAH FAWCETT-MAJOR'S LOOK.**

In the 1970s, the *60 MINUTES* team included *(clockwise from left)* Morley Safer, Dan Rather, and Mike Wallace. Don Hewitt *(bottom right)* was the television program's executive producer.

CHAPTER EIGHT

BREAKING THE MOLD:
STAGE AND SCREEN IN THE 1970s

S tage and screen stars of the 1970s broke the old enter-tainment mold. Advancing technology and a new openness about personal and political subjects led to exciting and creative television and movies.

■ TELEVISION NEWS

For many Americans, television was the sole source of daily news in the 1970s. Each of the three main national networks reported current events nightly. The popularity of network news programs made stars of the journalists who anchored them. NBC's John Chancellor and David Brinkley, ABC's Peter Jennings, and CBS's Walter Cronkite won universal respect for their balanced, intelligent work. Cronkite earned the nickname Old Iron Pants for his com-posure under pressure. From 1965 to 1995, Americans voted him the Most Trusted Man in America.

The television newsmagazine format developed in the 1970s to satisfy viewers who wanted more thorough TV news coverage. The United States' first national investi-gative reporting show, *60 Minutes*, had barely made waves in 1968. Station managers kept moving the show around until it followed Sunday football programming in 1976. By then Dan Rather had joined coanchors Morley Safer and Mike Wallace, and the show's ratings increased. Pub-lic broadcasting scored with a similar newsmagazine, *MacNeil/Lehrer Report*.

97

■ CABLE TELEVISION

Cable access and programming were limited during the early 1970s, so few homes had cable television. Program services sold specific shows to cable operators. Cable operators owned the means to deliver television signals to homes via cables. Operators sold both service and programming to individual customers. In the early 1970s, federal regulators limited cable topics to education and government and restricted cable services to local and rural markets.

After 1975 regulators let cable services and programming expand. Warner Communications introduced Nickelodeon and The Movie Channel in 1979. Getty Oil bankrolled the launch of Entertainment and Sports Programming Network (ESPN) the same year. Cable television grew quickly after these changes. In 1975 ten million cable subscriptions supported 3,506 cable systems. By 1985 nearly forty million subscribers supported 6,600 systems.

■ DYING BREEDS AND NEWCOMERS

Several types of TV shows faded during the 1970s. Westerns, a mainstay of the 1950s and 1960s, died by the beginning of the seventies. Period family dramas replaced the cowboys-and-Indians fare. *Little House on the Prairie*, about a pioneer family on the Great Plains, and *The Waltons*, about a large Virginia family during the Great Depression and World War II, were especially popular.

The TV series *THE WALTONS*, which aired from 1972 to 1981, was based on a popular 1960s novel and movie, which starred Henry Fonda and Maureen O'Hara.

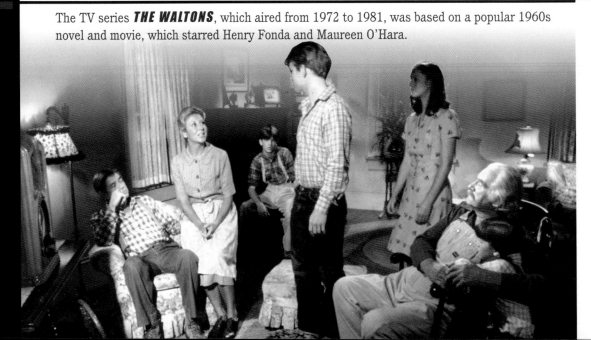

Variety shows with skits, singing, dancing, and comedy faded more slowly than westerns. A few variety shows of the 1960s, such as *The Carol Burnett Show* and *Laugh-In*, lasted into the 1970s. Creative variety shows often introduced new stars. In 1970 *The Flip Wilson Show* led its time segment in ratings. This newcomer was the first variety show hosted by an African American. Wilson, a comedian, introduced the singing group Tony Orlando and Dawn on one of his shows. This group soon began hosting the first multiethnic variety show. Husband-and-wife duo Sonny Bono and Cher (Cherilyn LaPierre) headlined another popular variety show, *The Sonny and Cher Show*. Cher delivered straight lines and a powerful contralto voice while her cheerful husband told jokes and harmonized. Clean-cut siblings Donny and Marie Osmond joked and sang their way to good ratings on *Donny and Marie*.

Family sitcoms, detective shows, and sports rounded out the 1970s TV diet. One popular show that mixed sitcom with variety and music was *The Partridge Family*. The show featured a widowed mother and her five talented children. Other popular sitcoms included *The Brady Bunch* and *The Jeffersons*. *Columbo* was a popular detective program.

Sonny Bono *(left)*, and Cher *(right)* perform together on their television variety program **THE SONNY AND CHER SHOW**.

1970s

100

AMERICA IN THE

New television shows reflected societal changes of the 1970s. *Mary Tyler Moore* depicted the first female lead who wasn't a mother, sidekick, or barmaid. Moore's single, successful thirtysomething character worked at a Minneapolis television station as a producer rather than a secretary. The show demonstrated that women can be successful and still lovable.

Some comedies attacked social barriers by poking fun at bigotry and shocking viewers into examining their own views. *All in the Family*'s central character, an uneducated white working-class bigot named Archie Bunker, broke all the rules. Bunker found life difficult in the freethinking 1970s. He spoke racial slurs and expressed every bias imaginable, including racism, sexism, and homophobia. Television censors wrung their hands, but viewers loved the show's honesty. Launched in 1971, *All in the Family* shot to first place in ratings and stayed there for five years.

The Vietnam War triggered another popular show, *M*A*S*H*. The program was based on Robert Altman's 1970 movie about a wacky Korean War army medical team. The show portrayed war's effects—homesickness, helplessness, violence, boredom, fear, and loneliness—through funny antics.

The most outrageous show born in the 1970s was *Saturday Night Live* (SNL). Producer and writer Lorne Michaels created sketches with guest hosts, musicians, and an ensemble cast that performed before a live New York audience. Segments spoofed politics, uncomfortable social situations, and current events through fake news, extreme silliness, and shocking behavior, such as pureeing a whole fish in a blender—and drinking it. The original cast (John Belushi, Gilda Radner, Dan Aykroyd, Garrett Morris, Chevy Chase, Laraine Newman, and Jane Curtin) called themselves the Not Ready for Prime Time Players. Many of them left the show after about five years for other television and movie careers, and new actors replaced them.

MARY TYLER MOORE appears in 1974 on the set of her highly successful sitcom, which ran from 1970 to 1977.

Public television tried to shed its stodgy image in the 1970s. Its award-winning program *Masterpiece Theatre* began introducing Americans to high-quality British drama in 1971. In November 1969, public TV had introduced an educational children's show called *Sesame Street*. This show grew very popular in the 1970s. *Sesame Street* revolutionized television programming for children. Instead of the usual white, middle-class children portrayed on television sitcoms, puppets Bert, Ernie, Big Bird, and more played with inner-city children and everyday workers on fictional Sesame Street. The show's writers wanted to encourage excitement and adventure from learning. So they named the street and show after the *Arabian Nights* magical saying "Open Sesame." *Sesame Street* entertained young children while sneaking in information about numbers, letters, and positive behavior. Innovative writers modeled the show after commercial television shows. They added fake ads to introduce concepts, such as: "Today's show is brought to you by the letter *m*."

Francesca Annis and Derek Smith star in a 1978 episode of public television's **MASTERPIECE THEATRE.** Over the years, the program has won thirty-three Primetime Emmys, seven International Emmys, and fifteen Peabody Awards.

1970s

AMERICA
IN THE

Joan Ganz Cooney (born 1929 in Arizona) wanted to improve the lives of others. She received her college degree in education and hoped to help children learn. But she decided a life in communications, including writing for television, could bring messages of change to more people.

In 1966 Cooney and Lloyd Morrisett, vice president of the charitable foundation Carnegie Corporation, discussed whether television could boost learning. At that time, most children's programs were boring documentaries or shows with clowns and other silly acts. To determine whether television had teaching potential, Cooney completed a report called "The Potential Uses of Television in Pre-School Education." Using ideas in this report, Cooney and Morrisett founded Children's Television Workshop (CTW) to create *Sesame Street*, a television show backed by Morrisett's foundation and other donors. Cooney envisioned a fast-paced show with enough interest to enhance preschool skills, particularly for disadvantaged children.

The resulting show starred a multiracial, multigenerational cast with equal roles for males and females. Cooney pitched her show to various public television networks that reached disadvantaged populations. The lively puppets and talented characters became an instant success. Cooney then created *The Electric Company* in 1971 to offer reading instruction to elementary-age students. She continued researching to identify other educational needs that television could address. CTW innovation resulted in several popular shows for adults and children, such as *Feeling Good* (1974), *The Best of Families* (1977), and *3-2-1 Contact* (1980). The shows and Cooney earned a steady stream of awards. Cooney retired as president of CTW in 1990 but continues to be a creative force in children's educational programming. Her vision of blending entertainment with learning raised the quality of children's television programming and boosted audiences for public television.

■ RISE OF BLOCKBUSTER MOVIES

For two decades, the movie industry had been losing its audience to television. In the 1970s, many baby boomers came of age and began looking away from their TVs for more diverse entertainment. The movie industry responded with breakthroughs in the type and quality of films they produced. In the film studies anthology *The Last Great American Picture Show*, critic David Thomson called the 1970s "The Decade When Movies Mattered." A new crop of young directors made films with creative plots and innovative special effects. "It was

> ## " It was the golden age of filmmaking because we were all single, ambitious, and we were in love with film. "

—Steven Spielberg, describing himself and fellow directors George Lucas,
Martin Scorsese, and Francis Ford Coppola in the 1970s

the golden age of filmmaking because we were all single, ambitious, and we were in love with film," Steven Spielberg said of himself and fellow directors George Lucas, Martin Scorsese, and Francis Ford Coppola.

Coppola scored his big break in 1972 with *The Godfather*. This violent, complex film—based on Mario Puzo's book by the same name—starred Marlon Brando as Mafia boss Don Vito Corleone and newcomer Al Pacino as Corleone's favorite son. The picture grossed eighty-six million dollars, breaking box-office records.

Spielberg's horror film *Jaws* (1975) began a new era in blockbuster movies. *Jaws* followed a scientist, police chief, and scruffy sailor on their journey to kill a shark terrorizing a seaside village. The film was the first high-budget, mass-market summer blockbuster. It earned three Academy Awards and thrust Spielberg into the limelight. Two years later, he held audiences spellbound again with *Close Encounters of the Third Kind*. This movie explored unidentified flying object (UFO) sightings and offered a kind view of alien beings.

103

Actors Richard Dreyfuss *(left)* and Robert Shaw star in the 1975 movie ***JAWS*** about a deadly great white shark that terrorizes the beaches of a fictional resort.

BREAKING THE MOLD: Stage and Screen in the 1970s

Lucas established his directorial career with the low-budget film *American Graffiti* (1973), which wove together the stories of small-town teenagers. Lucas then captured the delight of science-fiction fans with *Star Wars* (1977). This outer-space picture rocked the movie world with its special effects. Lucas's use of light, movement, and photography brought battle scenes between the evil Darth Vader and do-gooder Luke Skywalker to life. Lucas formed his own company, Industrial Light and Magic (ILM), to create special effects for *Star Wars*. ILM has since contributed to dozens of movies.

The Vietnam War inspired production of several war movies. *The Deer Hunter* (1978) and *Apocalypse Now* (1979) focused on soldiers' experiences overseas. Other films explored the aftermath of combat. *Taxi Driver* (1976) showed how war claims the minds and hearts of veterans, often causing insanity. *Coming Home* (1978) told the story of a wounded soldier trying to pick up the pieces of his life.

Hollywood began making movies aimed at black audiences in the 1970s. *Shaft* (1971) pioneered movies for and about African Americans. In this film, Richard Roundtree led a mostly black

From left: Mark Hamill, Carrie Fisher, and Harrison Ford star as Luke Skywalker, Princess Leia, and Han Solo in the 1977 blockbuster movie **STAR WARS.** Two sequels, three prequels, an animated movie, and a strong fan base followed the original movie.

The mob wanted Harlem back. They got Shaft... up to here.

SHAFT

SHAFT's his name. SHAFT's his game.

METRO·GOLDWYN·MAYER Presents "SHAFT" Starring RICHARD ROUNDTREE Co-Starring MOSES GUNN
Screenplay by ERNEST TIDYMAN and JOHN D. F. BLACK Based upon the novel by ERNEST TIDYMAN
Music by ISAAC HAYES Produced by JOEL FREEMAN Directed by GORDON PARKS METROCOLOR
R   MGM

Richard Roundtree starred as African American private detective John Shaft in the 1971 movie *SHAFT* and its two sequels.

cast as he played a fearless detective protecting the mean streets of Harlem. But the movie ushered in a decade of action films that negatively stereotyped black men and women and provided violent role models for black youth.

Meaty leading roles for women had once been rare. In the 1970s, they became more common. Jane Fonda earned her first Academy Award for playing a prostitute-turned-detective in *Klute* (1971). Fonda won her second Oscar in 1978 for playing a soldier's repressed wife in *Coming Home*. *Annie Hall* (1977) established Diane Keaton as a quirky and lovable character. Faye Dunaway led the cast of *Chinatown* (1974) on a dark family journey through murder, politics, and corruption in 1930s Los Angeles. Two years later, Dunaway earned an Oscar for playing an ambitious television producer in *Network*.

FAYE DUNAWAY stars in *Network* (1976), which earned four Academy Awards, including Best Actress for Dunaway.

Other popular movies highlighted real-life problems. In *One Flew Over the Cuckoo's Nest* (1975), Jack Nicholson played a convict trying to avoid prison by pretending to be insane. This hit movie made Nicholson a sought-after character actor. In the 1970s, Dustin Hoffman played a range of characters who explored issues of the times. *Little Big Man* (1970) cast Hoffman as a 121-year-old recalling his adoption and upbringing by Native Americans. Hoffman later played journalist Carl Bernstein with Robert Redford, who played Bob Woodward, in *All the President's Men* (1976). In *Kramer vs. Kramer* (1979), Hoffman played a father embroiled in a painful divorce and child custody battle.

In addition to realism, 1970s Hollywood produced its share of detective, feel-good, and horror movies. In 1971 Clint Eastwood starred as a hard-hitting detective in *Dirty Harry*. Four more Dirty Harry movies followed. In *Rocky* (1976), the first of six Rocky films, Sylvester Stallone played an underdog boxer who became successful. *The Exorcist* (1973) offered shameless gore and terror as two priests chased away demons inhabiting a little girl. The creepy *Carrie* (1976) provided similar demons and blood.

■ EVOLVING BROADWAY LIGHTS

During the 1960s, few musicals had been blockbusters in New York City's Broadway theater district. Then the antiwar rock opera *Hair* debuted in 1967. This new musical format helped fuel a theater turnaround. Rock musicals such as *The Me Nobody Knows* (1970) and *Jesus Christ Superstar* (1971) played for long runs on Broadway and in other major cities.

Rock musicals opened doors to more musical innovations. Shows by and about African Americans, such as *Purlie* (1970) and *The Wiz* (1975), put blacks at center stage. Musical story lines in *Company* (1970) and *Follies* (1971) explored relationships. Director Bob Fosse highlighted dance in *Chicago* (1975) and *Dancin'* (1978). *A Chorus Line* (1975) honored Fosse with a plot about a Broadway chorus audition with a demanding director. By the end of the decade, popular musicals turned edgy. For example, *The Best Little Whorehouse in Texas* (1978) sang about the real-life politics that led to closing of a well-known brothel.

Plays without music had a similar edge. *Equus* (1974) portrayed a psychiatrist treating a teenager's sexual fascination with horses. *Sweeney Todd: The Demon Barber of Fleet Street* (1973) told of a serial killer in 1800s London whose lover baked his victims into meat pies.

107

A CHORUS LINE is a Broadway show about Broadway. The show ran for more than six thousand performances (the longest run up to that time) and won nine Tony Awards.

"In the 1960s, one kind of music absorbed everything else. Now the universe of music is expanding on all fronts."

—*Columbia Records president Clive Davis, 1973*

Friends play music on a
RECORD PLAYER.

CHAPTER NINE

THERE'S A RIOT GOIN' ON:

MUSIC IN THE 1970s

Music fans of the 1970s heard it all: anger, love, rebellion, and experimentation. In the 1970s, music splintered into styles that mirrored the range of emotions expressed on the streets. The straightforward melodies and easygoing harmonies of the 1960s gave way to a hodgepodge of sounds. Rock mixed with disco and country. Jazz developed into rhythm and blues (R&B). Heavy metal and punk exploded with rage. Columbia Records president Clive Davis noted in 1973, "In the 1960s, one kind of music absorbed everything else. Now the universe of music is expanding on all fronts."

■ HOW MUSIC LOVERS LISTENED

Compact disc (CD) technology had been around for some time, but CDs were unavailable for public purchase. Seventies music fans listened to tunes on radios, record players, and 8-track tape players (devices for playing an early form of magnetic cassette tapes). As the decade wore on, compact cassette players and boom boxes gained in popularity. Boom boxes let listeners carry their music with them. They typically had a handle and contained an AM-FM radio, stereo speakers, and a compact cassette player. Boom boxes remained popular from about 1976 until the mid-1980s.

Radio stations sent signals over both AM broadcast systems and newly defined FM systems. FM radio quickly gained a reputation for better sound. Many AM station owners launched FM stations for varied programming and experimental music. By the close of the decade, FM ruled the radio airwaves.

◼ ENDINGS AND BEGINNINGS

Three legends left the U.S. music scene during the 1970s. The Beatles separated at the end of 1970. Band members Paul McCartney, John Lennon, George Harrison, and Ringo Starr then embarked on solo careers. After winning several Grammy Awards in 1971, duo Paul Simon and Art Garfunkel split too. Simon went on to explore music from around the world, while Garfunkel pursued an acting and solo career. Elvis Presley died in 1977.

Several 1960s music stars stayed popular by tailoring their music to 1970s rock fans who preferred livelier tunes. Neil Young, Carly Simon, Carole King, James Taylor, and Joni Mitchell wrote and sang brooding, personal songs. Other established groups, such as Chicago and Pink Floyd, experimented with horn sections and electric instruments. The British rock group Queen, which combined electric and symphonic instruments, was wildly popular in the late 1970s.

In 1970 British singer-songwriter Elton John debuted in the United States to rave reviews. He appeared before huge audiences in sequined, brightly colored outfits complete with his trademark oversize glasses. Always a showman, he sometimes performed handstands on his piano. John experienced his most successful years in the 1970s. He produced one hit album per year and a steady stream of hit singles, including "Rocket Man" and "Crocodile Rock."

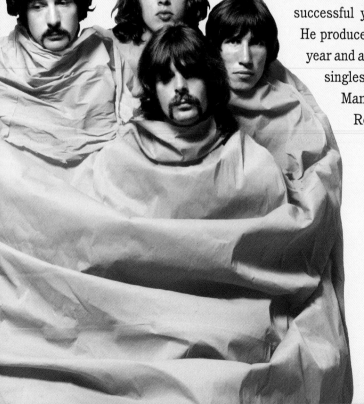

Popular **PINK FLOYD** band members *(left to right)* are Nick Mason, Dave Gilmour, Rick Wright, and Roger Waters.

isco began in New York City's black, gay, and Latin nightclubs. Singers such as Donna Summer and Barry White launched their careers singing disco tunes. After the movie *Saturday Night Fever* opened in 1977, the disco craze spread nationwide. The movie's lively songs—including several by Australia's Bee Gees—became hits along with the movie. Within a year, the sound track sold more than thirty million copies worldwide.

Disco reflected the self-obsession of the "me" decade. This flashy, high-energy dance music turned its back on political messages and melodic storytelling in favor of sensuality and seduction. To enjoy disco, men and women gathered in trendy dance clubs under blinking strobe lights. Thumping beats lured dancers onto the floor and into the arms of their partners.

At the close of the decade, nondisco artists recorded their versions of popular disco songs. The disco influence ushered

THE BEE GEES, a trio of brothers, were a disco sensation in the 1970s.

in dance-related films, such as *Fame* and *Flashdance*. But many listeners found disco music flashy and vacant compared with earlier music. In the 1980s, disco evolved into other forms of music and dance.

111

By the 1970s, rock musicians had perfected the art of spectacle. Mick Jagger, lead singer of the Rolling Stones, continued to prance across U.S. stages in skintight pants and low-cut tops. Punk rocker Patti Smith played air guitar while launching her 1975 album *Horses*. British singer David Bowie found a foothold in the United States when he invented Ziggy Stardust, his wacky alter ego. Ziggy Stardust sported a wild and glittery getup, tons of makeup, and blazing red hair.

SEX PISTOLS bassist Sid Vicious *(left)* and lead singer Johnny Rotten *(right at microphone)* were at the forefront of the 1970s punk music scene.

Many hard rockers went out of their way to shock audiences. Sex Pistols bassist Sid Vicious incorporated self-injury into his performances. KISS, Black Sabbath, and Led Zeppelin added outrageous costumes and wild stage acts. All screamed their songs to throbbing electric guitars and drums.

■ COUNTRY FARE

Country music found new fans during the late 1960s and 1970s. Lovers of the traditional "Nashville sound" listened to Willie Nelson, Johnny Cash, and Dolly Parton. Loretta Lynn sang about growing up poor but happy in "Coal Miner's Daughter." Merle Haggard cranked out country music's typical hard-luck songs, such as his ballad "Are the Good Times Really Over?"

But country music changed during the seventies. Waylon Jennings added brushed bass rhythms he'd learned from rocker Buddy Holly. Folksinger Bob Dylan explored country music influences with his rock group, The Band, as did John Denver with "Thank God I'm a Country Boy." Once disc jockeys had played country music only on country radio stations. Modern country tunes by popular stars appealed to broader audiences.

■ SOFTER SOUNDS

Many music lovers who preferred mellower sounds listened to easy-listening artists such as John Denver and the sibling duo Karen and Richard Carpenter. The Carpenters produced twelve top-ten singles between 1969 and 1983. They sold millions of records with their signature dreamy style. John Denver, formerly of the popular folk group the Chad Mitchell Trio, became a superstar when he started writing and recording his own songs during the 1970s. From the late sixties until his death in 1997, Denver produced fourteen gold and eight platinum albums. Denver was one of the first mainstream entertainers to embrace environmental messages in his music.

The decade produced its share of vocal divas. Barbra Streisand and Liza Minnelli, both popular in the 1960s, continued belting out new songs throughout the 1970s. Each acted and sang in popular movies. Minnelli earned an Oscar for her performance in *Cabaret* (1972) as a singer in Berlin during the rise of German Nazi dictator Adolf Hitler. Streisand won the same award a year later for playing the romantic lead opposite Robert Redford in *The Way We Were*.

For classical music fans, Chicago was an exciting place to live. The Chicago Symphony Orchestra, conducted by Sir Georg Solti, rose to unusual heights in 1971. That year the symphony booked its first European tour. The tour proved such a success that Chicagoans lined the streets to cheer the musicians in a welcome-home parade. "Now, everybody recognizes we have the best symphony in the world," said violinist Victor Aitay.

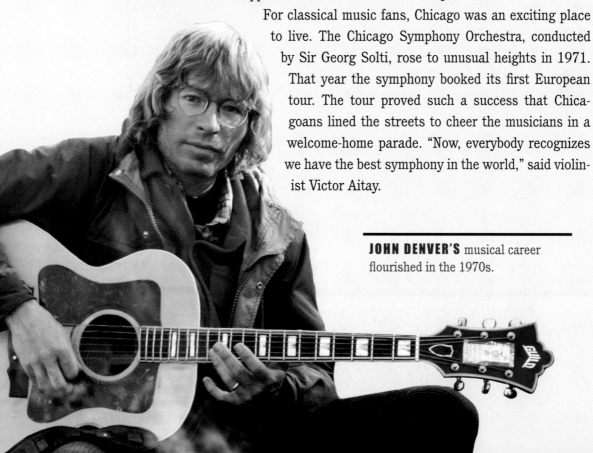

JOHN DENVER'S musical career flourished in the 1970s.

J ames Brown (1933–2006) was a singer, songwriter, bandleader, civil rights activist, and convict. He lived a full life, from growing up desperately poor in the segregated South to becoming one of the most influential R&B entertainers of all time.

After a troubled youth that included foster care, odd jobs, gambling, and jail time for armed robbery, Brown turned to music for survival. At the age of twenty, he joined a group called the Gospel Starlighters. He quickly became the group's headliner and helped the group, renamed the Famous Flames, change its focus to R&B. The group's first professional recording, "Please, Please, Please," reached number six on the R&B charts and launched Brown's career as a singer and bandleader.

Brown created the funk sound. His half-talking, half-singing vocals were an important forerunner of modern rap. Brown's lyrics, set to strong bass rhythms, touched on social and political problems of the 1960s and 1970s. "Heat the beat and the rest'll turn sweet" was his motto.

From his first recordings, Brown's songs topped R&B charts. His 1972 "Get on the Good Foot" gave Brown and his new group, the J.B.'s, their first gold record (one million in sales). Thereafter, Brown called himself the Godfather of Soul.

JAMES BROWN became known as the Godfather of Soul.

In the late 1970s, Brown's star power dimmed. But he continued to find new audiences, and he released hits in every decade even while battling addiction and personal problems. From 1988 to 1991, Brown served time in prison for domestic violence. After his release, the honors continued to flow. He won the Lifetime Achievement Award at the 1992 Grammy Awards. Just after his seventieth birthday in 2003, Brown was a recipient of the prestigious Kennedy Center Honors. He died on Christmas 2006.

■ BLACK BEATS

African American music took many forms in the 1970s. James Brown, the self-named Godfather of Soul, turned a mix of soul, gospel, and R&B into a novel style called funk. Brown influenced Sly and the Family Stone, a multiracial R&B band. Their 1968 single "Dance to the Music" had topped the charts in the United States and United Kingdom. The group went on to produce a string of hits during the next few years, each edgier than the last. The band's 1971 album *There's a Riot Goin' On* reflected members' personal conflicts and drug problems as well as the turmoil of a country at war.

Motown Records, a Detroit company founded by African American Berry Gordy in 1959, promoted popular soul music artists into the 1970s. Gordy had a knack for turning street singers and unknown bands into stars. Stevie Wonder, who had signed with Motown in 1961 at the age of eleven, found commercial and critical success in the 1970s. So did Marvin Gaye. Motown's last big act was the Jackson Five. Michael Jackson, the group's youngest singer, and his four older brothers pumped out six top-five singles in 1971.

Gordy tightly controlled his artists' music to conform to the "Motown sound." A typical Motown song used tambourine to accent the backbeat, melodic bass guitar, and a call-and-response style similar to gospel music. Gordy also controlled his artists' look and public image. Some Motown stars itched for more artistic freedom. Gaye left Gordy first and produced his own album, *What's Going On*, in 1971. He added conga drums to Gordy's pop beat and pleaded in his lyrics for an end to the Vietnam War and social problems such as drug abuse, political corruption, and pollution. Inspired by Gaye's success, Wonder and Jackson struck out on their own too.

An American family sets out for a BIKE RIDE in the 1970s.

CHAPTER TEN

BREAKTHROUGHS AND TRAGEDIES:
SPORTS IN THE 1970s

The 1970s sports scene reflected other aspects of society. Amateur athletes extended the new popular interest in healthy living to body fitness. And professional athletes found civil rights, women's rights, and turbulent politics affected their world of sports.

■ PSYCHED FOR FITNESS

To keep fit, many baby boomers filled yoga and aerobics classes. The more athletic tried endurance sports, such as jogging, swimming, and bicycling. In 1970, for the first time in decades, bicycles outsold cars. By 1973 bicycle sales doubled, and more than 50 percent were for adults. Six years later, almost one in three Americans owned a bicycle.

Several factors contributed to the surge in bicycling. Jogging strained the body, spurring millions of fitness seekers to either skip it or switch to cycling. Meanwhile, the United States began importing low-priced, lightweight ten-speed bicycles from France and Japan. Oil shortages and growing city traffic and air pollution made bicycling a logical choice for anyone concerned about the environment.

■ TENNIS CRAZE

In 1968 tennis organizations had abandoned the distinction between amateur and professional players. Talented players could earn a living at tennis without forfeiting the right to

117

Outdated views about women in sports lingered into the 1970s. Society never took women athletes seriously. Some people believed women were physically incompetent or that sports would harm female health.

As a result, girls found limited sports opportunities. Most school and community teams were reserved for boys. Women who competed professionally usually earned less money than their male peers. Sportswriters focused on men. They limited women's coverage to socially acceptable female sports, such as figure skating and gymnastics.

This situation changed when Congress passed the Education Amendments of 1972. Title IX of this act ordered schools receiving federal money to give girls the same opportunities as boys. The directive included sports opportunities. The new law meant that schools had to make teams, equipment, and all sports available to girls. In addition, the law championed the notion that girls could succeed if given the chance.

Many U.S. schools tried to block Title IX. Coaches claimed that spending limited resources on girls would end prized boys' teams. But the law stood, and schools began expanding sports programs for girls. In 1970 only 7.5 percent of college women participated in sports programs. By 1978 that amount jumped to 32 percent. Before the 1972 law, only one in twenty-seven high school girls played sports. Within twenty years, that ratio grew to one in three. Gradually females broke into mostly male arenas, such as basketball, hockey, and coaching. Athletic girls who were once told to watch or cheerlead began winning their own medals.

play in the sport's top tournaments. During the next few years, tennis transformed from a clubby game for English speakers to a televised sport with worldwide appeal. Local schools and recreation centers started offering tennis lessons. U.S. racket manufacturers doubled their sales between 1971 and 1973.

U.S. tennis players Chris Evert and Jimmy Connors became household names. Both helped popularize the two-handed backhand grip among U.S. players. Another top player, Arthur Ashe, earned his star power on and off the court.

In 1969 Ashe had been the top-ranked U.S. player. But South Africa's racist government had denied him a visa to play in the South African Open because he was black. Ashe used his status to protest the country's apartheid policies.

Apartheid was the name for South Africa's formal system of segregation and discrimination against nonwhites. Ashe demanded that South Africa be banned from the professional tennis circuit.

Ashe went on to become the first black player to win the men's singles at Wimbledon, the U.S. Open, and Australian Open—all top tennis competitions. A heart attack cut short his tennis career in 1979. He received blood transfusions during heart surgery, and in 1988, he discovered that one of his transfusions had given him acquired immunodeficiency syndrome (AIDS).

In retirement Ashe promoted broadening the youth appeal of tennis. He also continued his civil rights activism and called for greater availability of good health care. Among many other honors, Ashe was elected to the International Tennis Hall of Fame in 1985. He died in 1993. In 1997 the U.S. Tennis Association unveiled Arthur Ashe Stadium, its new main venue for the U.S. Open.

ARTHUR ASHE hits a backhand shot during the 1971 Wimbledon Lawn Tennis Championships in England.

The early 1970s were the golden age of tennis for men and women. But women still received lower pay than men did, and sexism was rampant.

Billie Jean King was at the top of her game then. In 1971 she won her second U.S. Open title and collected one hundred thousand dollars. King earned the highest annual fees of any female tennis player. The next year, she triumphed at the U.S. Open, French Open, and Wimbledon. The Associated Press named her Woman Athlete of the Year in 1967 and 1973. She was also the Sports Illustrated Sportsperson of the Year in 1972.

In 1973 former tennis champ Bobby Riggs challenged King to a tennis match. At the time, *Fortune* magazine called Riggs a "55-year-old tennis hustler who wore his chauvinism on his sleeve." Riggs believed he could beat the reigning female champ simply because he was male. Male athletes were superior, he claimed—"even those of advancing age."

King and Riggs arranged to compete for a winner-take-all purse of one hundred thousand dollars. The media billed the event as the Battle of the Sexes. Both players contributed to the media circus leading up to the match by sparring through reporters. Before the first game at the Houston Astrodome in Texas on September 20, 1973, King gave Riggs a live pig. The pig symbolized King's view that Riggs was a male chauvinist pig—a man who acted superior toward women.

Billie Jean King returns a shot at the net during her tennis match against Bobby Riggs in the 1973 BATTLE OF THE SEXES.

Once they began playing, however, King turned all business. She crushed Riggs in three straight sets. King was thrilled—not only for the win but for the statement it made on behalf of women athletes. "This is the culmination of 19 years of work," she said afterward. "Since the time [professional tennis] wouldn't let me in a picture because I didn't have on a tennis skirt, I've wanted to change the game around. Now it's here." After the match, King helped establish the Women's Tennis Association and Women's Sports Foundation. These groups helped ensure that women and girls received the same treatment as men in all sports.

■ OLYMPIC GAMES

The 1972 Summer Olympics in Munich, Germany, stood out for two reasons. One was the outstanding performance of U.S. swimmer Mark Spitz. Sports watchers had named Spitz the World Swimmer of the Year in 1969, 1971, and 1972. Fans expected him to be a front-runner at the 1972 Olympics, and he didn't disappoint them. Spitz became the first athlete to win seven gold medals at one Olympics: the 100- and 200-meter freestyle, 100- and 200-meter butterfly, and three relays. Olympic fame brought him seven million dollars in endorsement and acting contracts. His gold-medal record remained unsurpassed for thirty-six years.

Shortly after Spitz made history at the Olympics, tragedy occurred. A terrorist attack at Munich's Olympic Village (the athletes' living quarters) overshadowed his achievement. Six days before the close of the games, eight armed Palestinians murdered an Israeli athlete and coach and then took nine other Israeli team members hostage. German police later stormed the air base where the Palestinians held their hostages. In the shootout that followed, the terrorists killed all nine hostages. More than eighty thousand athletes and supporters attended a memorial service in the stadium. Competition stopped for twenty-four hours. After competition resumed, life went out of the games. Several teams and individuals withdrew. Many of the remaining athletes competed in a daze of grief and worry.

One of the Palestinian terrorists involved in the **KIDNAPPING AND MURDER OF ISRAELI ATHLETES** at the 1972 Summer Olympics in Germany appears on a hotel balcony.

The 1976 Summer Olympics in Montreal, Canada, produced its own drama. Twenty-eight African nations demanded that New Zealand's national rugby team be banned for having toured South Africa. When the International Olympic Committee refused this demand, the teams withdrew from the games in protest.

One highlight of competition among the remaining athletes was the U.S. boxing team. Sugar Ray Leonard, Leon Spinks, Michael Spinks, Leo Randolph, and Howard Davis each won a gold medal. This was the best U.S. Olympic boxing showing ever.

Another highlight of the competition was fourteen-year-old Romanian gymnast Nadia Comaneci. Comaneci received the first perfect score in Olympic gymnastics history. Then she repeated the feat six more times in Montreal. Her performance inspired thousands of U.S. girls to join gymnastics.

The achievement also launched her coach, Bela Karolyi, to international stardom. Karolyi soon defected to the United States from Communist Romania and opened a gym. He later led the 1988 and 1992 U.S. Olympic teams to victory. Comaneci and Karolyi helped popularize the idea of tiny young gymnasts. These types of athletes performed feats with their bodies that seemed impossible before the 1970s. But these achievements brought problems. The emphasis on size led many gymnasts to eating disorders, and some coaches pushed their athletes to extremes.

NADIA COMANECI performs on the balance beam during the 1976 Olympic Games in Montreal. She earned a perfect score in this event and six others.

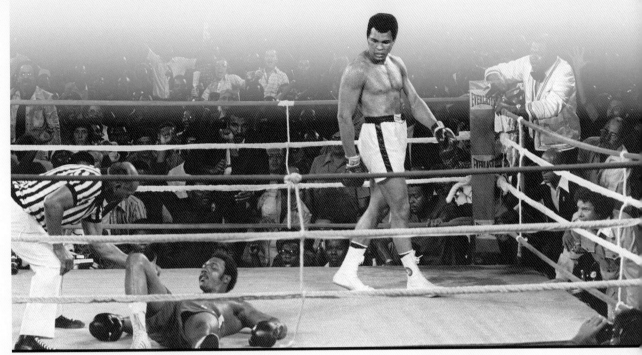

George Foreman was down for the count in round eight of the 1974 bout with **MUHAMMAD ALI**.

■ FIGHTER OF THE CENTURY

Boxer Muhammad Ali had turned professional after winning Olympic gold in 1960. He won the professional heavyweight title in 1964, and most people considered him the world's greatest boxer. But he ran into trouble that prevented him from boxing. He'd become a champ who couldn't box. Ali had refused to join the military during the Vietnam War draft. When asked why, he explained that his Islamic faith forbade it and said, "I ain't got no quarrel with them Vietcong." The courts branded Ali a draft dodger (a grave federal crime), and in 1967, the state boxing commissions suspended his licenses one by one. To clear his name and return to boxing, Ali took his case all the way to the Supreme Court.

In 1970 the New York boxing commission reinstated Ali's license. He hoped to regain his title by fighting the new heavyweight champ, Joe Frazier, in the 1971 Fight of the Century. Neither man had ever lost a pro fight. Frazier dealt Ali his first defeat. But a few months later, Ali won his Supreme Court battle. Ali reclaimed his boxing title in 1974 by knocking out reigning heavyweight champ George Foreman. Ali's lightning-fast punches, fancy footwork, and taunting enlivened the match. Many reporters claimed this fight confirmed Ali's self-styled nickname, the Greatest of All Time.

❝ I ain't got no quarrel with them Vietcong. ❞

—*Muhammad Ali, 1967, explaining his refusal to join the military during the Vietnam War draft*

■ BASEBALL AND SOFTBALL

During the 1970s, both softball and baseball caught the nation's attention. In 1976 tennis star Billie Jean King, softball legend Joan Joyce, and others founded the International Women's Professional Softball Association. The league featured teams from ten major U.S. cities. It made a big splash but lasted only four seasons before dying due to inadequate funds and facilities.

The 1970s produced some of baseball's biggest stars. Pete Rose played first, second, and third base and outfielder—mostly for the Cincinnati Reds—and achieved All-Star status in each position. He helped the Reds win World Series championships in 1975 and 1976.

Hank Aaron played for the Milwaukee Braves (1954–1965), Atlanta Braves (1966–1974), and Milwaukee Brewers (1975–1976). He broke many hitting records in the 1970s. Most notably, he set the record for most career home runs. He held this record and the record for most career extra base hits and total bases for thirty-three years. Aaron was elected to the National Baseball Hall of Fame in 1982 and became one of the first African Americans to reach Major League Baseball's top management.

The umpire declares Cincinnati Reds player **PETE ROSE** safe at third base during a game against the New York Yankees in the 1976 World Series.

New Jersey Nets player **DOCTOR J** drives past an opponent during a 1976 game.

■ BASKETBALL

Basketball entered the 1970s with great excitement among its fans. In 1967 the American Basketball Association (ABA) had started to rival the twenty-year-old National Basketball Association (NBA). The ABA created additional competition for players and fans, and the leagues eventually merged into the NBA in 1976.

Many of the NBA's top players, including forward Julius Erving, came from the ABA. Erving, nicknamed Doctor J, stole the show with his hard-driving style. During his sixteen professional seasons, Erving became one of basketball's three top career scorers, averaging more than twenty points and twenty rebounds per game.

College basketball, particularly from UCLA, provided top picks for the NBA. Between 1963 and 1975, UCLA took ten national championships. The best UCLA player to turn professional was Kareem Abdul-Jabbar. He led the Milwaukee Bucks to a 1971 NBA title and the Los Angeles Lakers to five NBA titles.

By the late 1970s, interest in the NBA lagged. Two college players, forward Larry Bird of Indiana State University and guard Earvin "Magic" Johnson of

Los Angeles Laker **MAGIC JOHNSON** *(left)* rips a rebound off the boards from Boston Celtic **LARRY BIRD** *(right)*.

Michigan State University, injected life into the game. The two caught the country's attention at the 1979 national college championship. Both went on to revive the NBA. Bird led the Boston Celtics to three NBA titles, and Johnson helped the Lakers win five NBA championships.

Females experienced the most dramatic changes in basketball. In 1971 rules changed to make the women's game about the same as men's. The greatest change for female athletes was Title IX. Between this new anti-discrimination law and the new rules, women's basketball flourished. In 1971 the first national college basketball tournament for women began. Five years later, the Olympics added a six-team women's basketball event. U.S. women finally had somewhere to go with their basketball talent beyond local and college teams.

Two standouts for the 1976 U.S. Olympic team were Ann Meyers and Nancy Lieberman. Meyers continued to sharpen her skills as the first woman to sign with the all-male NBA. Lieberman became the youngest basketball player to earn an Olympic medal when the United States took home the silver. During the late 1970s, she continued to play basketball at Old Dominion University in Virginia.

ANN MEYERS shows off her number 15 jersey for the NBA team Indiana Pacers. She signed with the Pacers as a free agent for fifty-thousand dollars but eventually was not chosen for the final squad.

In 1978 the Women's Pro Basketball League (WBL) began. The WBL established eight teams to compete professionally. Although the league fizzled in three years, it helped women's basketball grow.

■ SOCCER

One man singlehandedly popularized soccer in the United States. Edison Arantes do Nascimento (better known by his nickname, Pelé), was Brazil's top player from 1957 until 1972. He won his first World Cup tournament at the age of seventeen and continued to dazzle the world on two more World Cup winning teams.

Pelé retired from Brazilian soccer in 1972. He joined the New York Cosmos in 1975. He received $2.8 million for a three-year contract. This was a huge amount at the time—especially for U.S. soccer, which was not very popular. Pelé's presence boosted average match attendance from 7,600 fans in 1975 to 13,600 in 1977. When Pelé's Cosmos contract ended, he retired to spread the joys of soccer worldwide. By then fans considered him the greatest soccer player in the history of the game.

PELÉ played for the New York Cosmos soccer team from 1975 to 1977.

Vice-presidential candidate GERALDINE FERRARO shakes hands with
supporters at a San Francisco rally in 1984. Ferraro, the first female candidate
for the position, ran beside Democratic presidential candidate Walter Mondale.
The duo lost the race to Ronald Reagan and George H. W. Bush.

BRIDGE TO THE

"ME ... ME ... ME ..." DECADE

The 1970s provided an exciting transition from the hippie-influenced 1960s to the conservative 1980s. Many ideas still considered extreme in 1970 became mainstream by 1980. Civil rights expanded to include all minorities. Women could finally call themselves "Ms." to avoid being defined by their marital status, and government worked to pass the Equal Rights Amendment. Homosexuals and people with disabilities pushed to be heard and to gain their rightful place in society. Various ethnic minorities—blacks, Native Americans, and immigrants—found their voices. Although clashes still happened over quotas, birth control, and busing, minority rights made major breakthroughs.

Science experienced great leaps into the future. Earth Day signaled a drastic change in public attitudes about the environment. Saving the environment took center stage on local, national, and global levels for the first time. The U.S. government banned dangerous chemicals and attempted to limit nuclear weapons. Even NASA developed reusable spacecraft. As new studies warned against the future risk of doing nothing to preserve Earth, more people understood that these steps taken in the 1970s were only the beginning of the task of saving the planet.

The most exciting news of the decade was the end of the Vietnam War. During the early 1970s, the war overwhelmed

129

Young people used to speaking out continued to test social limits with experimental lifestyles, unusual fashion, and loud music.

politics government, the arts, and everyone's thoughts. After the war ended, the nation felt freer to focus on other issues. Young people used to speaking out continued to test social limits with experimental lifestyles, unusual fashion, and loud music. Many youths viewed everyone over thirty as the enemy. Older Americans shook their heads, hoping this phase would end. And it did.

Still, challenges continued. President Carter swooped into office to clean up Nixon's scandals. He arranged the first lasting peace between Egypt and Israel. But the Iranian revolution and taking of U.S. hostages doomed his presidency. His difficulty freeing the hostages allowed Ronald Reagan to win the 1980 presidential election.

PRESIDENT RONALD REGAN works at his desk in the Oval Office in the 1980s.

Reagan's administration eventually slowed or reversed many hard-won social and political gains from the previous decade. He and the conservatives who supported him took a hard line against other nations as well as U.S. citizens. The government pulled back on social programs, making life rougher for poor people and farmers. The easy flow of money that had built a solid middle class in the 1960s slowed to a trickle into the 1980s. The average family found money tight.

Unlike ordinary Americans, business executives thrived as Reagan reduced regulations on commerce. Big companies bought smaller ones, creating giant corporations. Their leaders amassed huge sums of money, expanding the population of millionaires. Businesses encouraged the public to buy, buy, buy. The growing advertising industry enticed Americans to amass as many goods as possible. The extreme emphasis on sales and money caused novelist Tom Wolfe, who had called the 1970s the "me" decade, to dub the 1980s the "Me . . . Me . . . Me . . ." decade.

TIMELINE

1970
- Americans celebrate the first Earth Day.
- Congress passes the Clean Air Act.
- Richard Nixon creates the Environmental Protection Agency (EPA).
- Nixon orders a U.S. invasion of Cambodia.
- National Guardsmen shoot protesters at Kent State University in Ohio.
- The National Organization for Women holds Women's Strike for Equality march in New York City.

1971
- The *New York Times* publishes portions of the Pentagon Papers.
- The Nixon administration creates the secret Plumbers unit and devises an enemies list.
- Plumbers burglarize the office of Daniel Ellsberg's psychiatrist.
- Congress bans cigarette advertising on radio and television.

1972
- Nixon's Plumbers break into the Democratic National Committee headquarters at the Watergate complex in Washington, D.C.
- EPA bans the cancer-causing pesticide DDT.
- Nixon makes a historic trip to China.
- Congress passes Equal Rights Amendment (ERA) and Title IX in support of women's rights.
- Eight armed Palestinians murder eleven Israeli Olympic team members in the Munich massacre.

1973
- U.S. involvement in the Vietnam War ends.
- Arab nations stop selling oil to the West, sparking an energy crisis.
- The U.S. Senate convenes a committee to investigate the Watergate break-in.
- NASA launches the space station Skylab.
- *Roe v. Wade* establishes a woman's right to have an abortion.
- Congress passes the Rehabilitation Act to guarantee fair access to federally funded programs for people with disabilities.
- Chicago's Sears Tower becomes the world's tallest building.

1974
- The House Judiciary Committee approves three articles to impeach President Nixon.
- Nixon resigns, and Gerald Ford assumes the presidency.
- Ford pardons Nixon.

1975
- Communist forces win the Vietnam War.
- The United States and Soviet Union cooperate in the Apollo-Soyuz test in space for the first time.
- Congress passes a law requiring public schools to provide free, appropriate, integrated education for students with disabilities.
- The movie *Jaws* launches a new era of blockbusters.

1976
- Jimmy Carter wins the presidential election.
- Alex Haley publishes his groundbreaking book *Roots*.
- Nadia Comaneci receives the first perfect score in Olympic gymnastics history.
- *A Chorus Line* opens on Broadway.

1977
- Carter unconditionally pardons draft evaders and military deserters.
- The first revision of tax codes in thirty years passes, increasing payments by wealthy individuals.
- Carter signs a major amendment to the Clean Air Act, strengthening air quality standards.
- Oil starts flowing through the Trans-Alaska Pipeline.
- The movie *Saturday Night Fever* starts a nationwide disco craze.

1978
- Toxic chemical pollution and related sickness in Love Canal, New York, becomes a national media event.
- Congress bans use of chlorofluorocarbon propellants, refrigerants, and cleaning solvents.
- Congress votes to extend ratification of the ERA.
- The American Indian Movement marches from San Francisco to Washington, D.C., to protest forced removal of Native Americans from their homelands.
- Frank Gehry designs his distinctive home in Santa Monica, California.

1979
- President Carter, Menachem Begin, and Anwar el-Sadat meet in Washington to sign the Israel-Egypt Peace Treaty.
- An accident at Three Mile Island nuclear power plant in Pennsylvania raises awareness of the risks of nuclear power.
- Islamic revolutionaries overthrow Iranian leader Shah Mohammad Reza Pahlavi, and cleric Ayatollah Ruholla Khomeini claims leadership.
- Iranians seize sixty-six hostages from the U.S. Embassy in Tehran and hold fifty-two of them for the next fourteen months.
- Judy Chicago completes her feminist art masterpiece *The Dinner Party*.

SOURCE NOTES

5   John Kennedy, "Text of Kennedy's Inaugural Outlining Policies on World Peace and Freedom," *New York Times*, January 21, 1961.

12 Barry Denenberg, *Voices from Vietnam* (New York: Scholastic, 1999), 176.

12 Ibid.

13 Rita Mae Brown, *Rita Will: Memoir of a Literary Rabble-Rouser* (New York: Bantam, 1997), 266.

15 Walter LaFeber, *America, Russia, and the Cold War 1945–1984* (New York: Alfred A. Knopf, 1985), 263.

15 Jim Hougan, *Secret Agenda: Watergate, Deep Throat and the CIA* (New York: Random House, 1984), 36.

16 Harold Evans, *The American Century* (New York: Alfred A. Knopf, 2000), 553.

16 Ibid.

19 LaFeber, 271.

19–20 Evans, 570.

20 Ibid.

23 Arthur Schlesinger Jr., ed., *The Almanac of American History* (New York: Barnes & Noble Books, 1993), 580.

23 Gerald Ford, "Gerald R. Ford: Address on Taking the Oath of the U.S. Presidency," *American Rhetoric*, n.d., http://www.americanrhetoric.com/speeches/geraldfordpresidentialoath.html (October 20, 2008).

25 Gerald Strober and Deborah Strober, *Nixon: An Oral History of His Presidency* (New York: HarperCollins, 1994), 478.

26 Ibid., 483, 486.

30 LaFeber, 285.

30 Strober and Strober, 486.

30 Jimmy Carter, *Keeping Faith* (New York: Bantam Books, 1982), 18.

31 Shirley Chisholm, *Unbought and Unbossed* (New York: Houghton Mifflin, 1972), 71.

31 Ibid., 12.

32 Evans, 611.

32 Ibid.

34 Carter, 403.

34 Ibid.

34 Ibid., 437.

35 Mike Wallace, *Between You and Me: A Memoir* (New York: Hyperion, 2005), 129.

36 Baqer Moin, *Khomeini: Life of the Ayatollah* (London: I. B. Tauris, 1999), 227–228.

37 Carter, 459.

40 Gaylord Nelson, "We Are Not Just Toying with Nature," *Progressive*, January 1999, 36–39.

44 H. W. Wilson, *Current Biography Yearbook: 1983* (New York: H. W. Wilson, 1983), 42.

44 Ibid.

44 L. B. Taylor Jr., *For All Mankind: America's Space Programs of the 1970s and Beyond* (New York: Dutton, 1974), 10.

52 David Frum, *How We Got Here: The 70's* (New York: Basic Books, 2000), 25.

52 Ibid.

54 Schlesinger, 603.

59 Loretta Britten, ed., *Time of Transition: The 70s* (Alexandria, VA: Time-Life Books, 1998), 83.

60 Elaine Tyler May, *Pushing the Limits: American Women 1940–1961* (New York: Oxford University Press, 1994), 145.

61 Strober and Strober, 64–65.

62 NOW, "Frequently Asked Questions," *National Organization for Women*, n.d., http://www.now.org/organization/faq.html (October 20, 2008).

62 Evans, 597.

63 Glenda Riley, Inventing the American Woman: An Inclusive History (Arlington Heights, IL: Harlan Davidson, 1986), 135.

63 Evans, 597.

75 Brown, 228.

75 *New York Times*, "4 Policemen Hurt in 'Village' Raid; Melee Near Sheridan Square Follows Action at Bar," June 29, 1969.

76 *New York Post*, "Village Raid Stirs Melee" June 28, 1969.

77 Evans, 601.

80 E. Howard Hunt, *American Spy: My Secret History in the CIA, Watergate and Beyond* (Hoboken, NJ: John Wiley and Sons, 2007), 177.

80 Ibid.

83 Paula Guran, "Joyce Carol Oates: The Gothic Queen." *Dark Echo*, September 1999, http://www.darkecho.com/darkecho/horroronline/oates.html (October 20, 2008).

85 Judy Blume, "Judy Blume Talks about Censorship," *Judy Blume on the Web*, n.d., http://judyblume.com/censorship.php (October 20, 2008).

88 Norma Broude and Mary D. Garrard, eds., *The Power of Feminist Art: The American Movement of the 1970s, History and Impact* (New York: Harry N. Abrams, 1994), 16.

88 Ibid., 146.

89 Judy Chicago, "Timeline," *Judy Chicago*, n.d., http://www.judychicago.com/?p=timeline (October 20, 2008).

89 Judy Chicago, *The Dinner Party: A Symbol of Our Heritage* (New York: Anchor Books, 1979), 12.

89 Ibid., 13.

90 Adrienne Drell, ed., *20th Century Chicago: 100 Years, 100 Voices* (Chicago: Sports Publishing, 2000), 161.

94 Mark Schmidt, ed., *The 1970s* (San Diego: Greenhaven Press, 2000), 219.

94 Ibid.

103 Britten, 176.

103 Ibid.

108 Ibid., 111.

109 Ibid.

113 Drell, 154.

115 Britten, 118.

120 Gooding Judson, "The Tennis Industry," *Fortune*, June 1973, 126.

120 Joe Layden, *Women in Sports: The Complete Book on the World's Greatest Female Athletes* (Santa Monica, CA: General Publishing Group, 1997), 134.

120 Ibid.

123 George Plimpton, "Heroes and Icons: Muhammad Ali," *Time.com*, June 14, 1999, http://www.time.com/time/time100/heroes/profile/ali03.html (October 20, 2008).

123 Ibid.

SELECTED BIBLIOGRAPHY

Alonso, Harriet Hyman. *Peace as a Women's Issue*. Syracuse, NY: Syracuse University Press, 1993. This book offers a thorough history of the U.S. feminist peace movement during the 1800s and 1900s.

Bailey, Harry A., and Jay M. Shafritz. *The American Presidency: Historical and Contemporary Perspectives*. Chicago: Dorsey Press, 1988. The authors discuss the role of the U.S. president, focusing on Richard Nixon.

Caplow, Theodore, Louis Hicks, and Ben J. Wattenberg. *The First Measured Century: An Illustrated Guide to Trends in America, 1900–2000*. Washington, DC: AEI Press, 2001. The title offers a complete statistical profile of the modern United States. It contains scores of graphs and figures that illustrate U.S. trends in all aspects of society, from the economy to government to social issues.

Carter, Jimmy. *An Hour Before Daylight: Memories of a Rural Boyhood*. New York: Simon & Schuster, 2001. In this memoir, President Carter describes his Depression-era childhood in rural Georgia.

Chadwick, Whitney. *Women, Art, and Society*. London: Thames and Hudson, 2002. Unlike most art books, which focus on male artists, this book captures the quantity and quality of female artists in Europe and North America from the Middle Ages to the twenty-first century.

Felder, Deborah G. *A Century of Women: The Most Influential Events in 20th Century Women's History*. Secaucus, NJ: Carol Publishing Group, 1999. The author of this book describes the key events and people of the women's movement through each decade of the 1900s.

Gottlieb, Sherry Gershon. *Hell No We Won't Go! Resisting the Draft during the Vietnam War*. New York: Viking, 1991. In this collection, men who resisted the Vietnam War draft for both moral and personal reasons tell their stories. In addition to many ordinary people, the author also interviewed actor Richard Dreyfus and boxer Muhammad Ali.

Jaeger, Paul T., and Cynthia Ann Bowman. *Understanding Disability: Inclusion, Access, Diversity, and Civil Rights*. Westport, CT: Praeger Publishing, 2005. This title helps readers understand the lives, limitations, and rights of people with disabilities.

Payne, Barbara, ed. *Eyewitness to the 20th Century*. Washington, DC: National Geographic Society, 1998. Trends, trivia, and photographs highlight this trip through the twentieth century for young adults.

136

Schmidt, Mark, ed. *The 1970s*. San Diego: Greenhaven Press, 2000.
This edition is a collection of essays by different authors about defining events of the 1970s.

Schulman, Bruce J. *The Seventies: The Great Shift in American Culture, Society, and Politics*. New York: Free Press, 2001.
This title examines political, cultural, social, and religious changes in the 1970s.

Smith, Lissa, ed. *Nike Is a Goddess: The History of Women in Sports*. New York: Atlantic Monthly Press, 1998.
This rich overview covers significant female athletes and sports events throughout the last century.

Steinem, Gloria. *Outrageous Acts and Everyday Rebellions*. New York: Holt, Rinehart and Winston, 1983.
In this collection of personal essays, Steinem tells stories that illustrate society's false images of and expectations for women. She also suggests ways women can combat these false roles and avoid being limited by them.

Walther, Ingo, ed. *Art of the 20th Century*. Vol. 2. New York: Taschen, 1998.
This volume provides an overview of art trends in the 1900s and the artists who participated in them.

White, Theodore. *The Making of the President, 1972*. New York: Atheneum, 1973.
This historian documents the presidency and downfall of Richard Nixon.

TO LEARN MORE

Books

Brill, Marlene Targ. *Winning Women in Basketball*. Hauppauge, NY: Barron's Educational Series, 2000.
This title offers the history of women in basketball and interviews with four key players.

Gherman, Beverly. *Jimmy Carter*. Minneapolis: Twenty-First Century Books, 2004.
This young adult biography recounts the life of the thirty-ninth U.S. president.

Giblin, James Cross, ed. *The Century That Was: Reflections on the Last One Hundred Years*. New York: Atheneum, 2000.
Each of eleven well-known children's authors focus on one aspect of life during the twentieth century.

Gourley, Catherine. *Ms. and the Material Girls: Perceptions of Women from the 1970s through the 1990s*. Minneapolis: Twenty-First Century Books, 2008.
This title in the Images and Issues series discusses the social and political representations of American women during the 1970s through the 1990s.

Levy, Debbie. *The Vietnam War*. Minneapolis: Twenty-First Century Books, 2004.
Readers can get information about the Vietnam War, from a brief description of the region's history and the U.S involvement in the conflict through the signing of the Paris Peace Accords in 1973 and the fall of Saigon in 1975.

Mantell, Paul. *Arthur Ashe: Young Tennis Champion*. New York: Aladdin, 2006.
This biography covers Ashe's life from his childhood in segregated Richmond, Virginia, to international tennis stardom. Along the way, he broke several color barriers and captured the hearts of people around the world.

Roberts, Selene. *A Necessary Spectacle: Billie Jean King, Bobby Riggs, and the Tennis Match That Leveled the Game*. New York: Crown, 2005.
Roberts sheds light on the childhoods of Riggs and King before Title IX. She also discusses the importance of King's victory for future female players.

Sherman, Josepha. *The Cold War*. Minneapolis: Twenty-First Century Books, 2004.
This book covers the troubled relations between the United States and the Soviet Union from the birth of the Soviet Union in 1922 to its breakup in 1991.

Winget, Mary Mueller. *Gerald R. Ford*. Minneapolis: Twenty-First Century Books, 2007.
This is the story of how Ford went from soldier to congressman and unexpectedly rose to vice president and president of the United States.

Films

Afros, Macks, 'n Zodiacs. Vol. 1, *A Compilation of Some of the Best Black Action Films of the 1970s*. VHS. Seattle: Something Weird Video, 1995.
This video offers an analysis of black action films that began in the 1970s.

American Musical Theater in the 1970s. VHS. Chicago: Educational Audio Vision, 1986.
This film shows highlights from the most popular musicals of the 1970s.

Nationally Televised Speeches of Jimmy Carter. VHS. Atlanta: Jimmy Carter Library, 1992.
This video is a good choice for presidential history buffs who want to review Carter's speeches and their content.

Websites

American Cultural History: 1970–1979
http://kclibrary.nhmccd.edu/decade70.html
This website, maintained by Lone Star College Kingwood Library in Texas, offers an overview of U.S. history and culture during the 1970s. It discusses art and architecture; literature; education; fads and fashion; technology; events and people; music; theater, film, and television; and sports. The website includes dozens of links and suggested readings.

America's Story
http://www.americaslibrary.gov
The "Jump Back in Time" page on this website includes biographies of famous Americans, original historic documents, and discussions about different periods in U.S. history.

Gerald R. Ford Presidential Library and Museum
http://www.fordlibrarymuseum.gov/
This website offers information about Ford, his presidency, and the presidential exhibits and documents housed in the Grand Rapids, Michigan, museum and the Ann Arbor library. The website also provides online access to many documents and photos from Ford's presidency.

Jimmy Carter Library and Museum
http://www.jimmycarterlibrary.org
This site provides information about the thirty-ninth U.S. president, including his life before 1976 and his activities since retiring.

SELECTED 1970S CLASSICS

Books

Haley, Alex. *Roots: The Saga of an American Family*. Garden City, NY: Doubleday, 1976.
The author traces his family's African and African American ancestry back to his great-great-great-great-grandfather Kunta Kinte, an African tribesman who was sold into slavery.

Morrison, Tony. *Song of Solomon*. New York: Knopf, 1977.
This novel follows Macon "Milkman" Dead III on his quest to discover his identity through his ancestors. It was chosen as an Oprah Book Club pick in 1996.

Segal, Erich. *Love Story*. New York: Harper & Row, 1970.
Segal wrote this novel to accompany his screenplay of the popular movie of the same name, both released in 1970. In this romance story, two young lovers (played in the movie by Ali MacGraw and Ryan O'Neal) from opposite sides of the tracks try to make a life together despite financial woes and terminal illness.

Films

The Godfather. VHS. Hollywood, CA: Paramount, 1972.
Marlon Brando plays an aging leader of a powerful crime family who wants his reluctant son, played by Al Pacino, to take over.

Jaws. VHS. Universal City, CA: Universal Studios, 1975.
This is director Steven Spielberg's groundbreaking thriller about a white shark terrorizing a small seaside village—and the men (played by Richard Dreyfus, Roy Scheider, and Robert Shaw) trying to stop it.

Star Wars. Los Angeles: Twentieth-Century Fox, 1977.
Mark Hamill, Carrie Fisher, and Harrison Ford star in this space adventure about a fictional galaxy in the grip of a battle between the forces of good and evil.

1970s ACTIVITY

Identify six to ten things in your own life or family history that relate to the 1970s. (To start your thinking, consider your grandparents' or neighbors' lives; family antiques or collections; your house or buildings in your neighborhood; favorite movies, books, songs, or TV shows; or places you've visited.) Use photographs, mementos, and words to create a print or computer scrapbook of your 1970s connections.

PHOTO ACKNOWLEDGMENTS

The images in this book are used with the permission of: © John Olson/Time & Life Pictures/Getty Images, p. 3; Abbie Rowe, National Park Service, John F. Kennedy Library, pp. 4–5; Library of Congress, pp. 6 (LC-DIG-ppmsca-03128), 31 (LC-DIG-ppmsc-01264); AP Photo, pp. 9, 12, 17, 20, 37, 38–39, 41, 43, 53, 55, 71 (both), 72, 77, 78–79, 124, 126; Nixon Presidential Library & Museum, pp. 10–11; © John Filo/Premium Archive/Getty Images, p. 13; © Michael Abramson/Time & Life Pictures/Getty Images, pp. 14, 140 (left); © Pictorial Parade/Hulton Archive/Getty Images, p. 15; © Keystone/Hulton Archive/Getty Images, p. 18; © Bill Eppridge/Time & Life Pictures/Getty Images, p. 19; © AFP/Getty Images, pp. 21, 35, 45, 122, 140 (right); © Bill Pierce/Time & Life/Getty Images, pp. 23, 128–129; Courtesy Gerald R. Ford Library, pp. 24–25; © Rolls Press/Popperfoto/Getty Images, p. 26; © Bettmann/CORBIS, pp. 27, 82, 85, 120; © Dirck Halstead/Liaison/Getty Images, p. 28; © US Navy/Time & Life Pictures/Getty Images, p. 29; © Hulton Archive/Getty Images, pp. 30, 111; Jimmy Carter Library, p. 33; Wisconsin Historical Society, WHi-48015, p. 40; © Joe Traver/Liaison/Getty Images, p. 42; © SSPL/The Image Works, p. 46; © Santi Visalli Inc./Hulton Archive/Getty Images, p. 48; © Lambert/Hulton Archive/Getty Images, pp. 50–51, 61; AP Photo/Marty Lederhandler, pp. 56–57; AP Photo/Frank Johnston, Pool, p. 58; © Bill Ray/Time & Life Pictures/Getty Images, p. 59; The Schlesinger Library, Radcliffe Institute, Harvard University, p. 60; © JP Laffont/Sygma/CORBIS, p. 62; Reprinted by permission of *Ms.* magazine, © 1972, p. 64; © Cynthia Macadams/Time & Life Pictures/Getty Images, pp. 65, 89, 140 (center); © William Albert Allard/National Geographic/Getty Images, p. 67; © Lee Lockwood/Time & Life Pictures/Getty Images, p. 69; AP Photo/Walt Zeboski, p. 70; © Fred W. McDarrah/Premium Archive/Getty Images, p. 75; © Keystone/Consolidated News Pictures/Hulton Archive/Getty Images, p. 81; © Alex Gotfryd/CORBIS, p. 83; Ozier Muhammad/Ebony Collection via AP Images, p. 84; © 2009 Judy Chicago/Artists Rights Society (ARS), New York. Photo © Donald Woodman, pp. 86–87; Faith Ringgold, For the Woman's House, 1971, oil on canvas, 96 x 96, Collection of NYC Rikers Island, © Faith Ringgold 1971, p. 88; © 2009 Calder Foundation/Artists Rights Society (ARS), New York. Photograph © Bettmann/CORBIS, p. 90; © Susan Wood/Hulton Archive/Getty Images, p. 91; © Topham/The Image Works, p. 92; Paramount/The Kobal Collection/Bower, Holly, p. 93; © Henry Groskinsky/Time & Life Pictures/Getty Images, p. 95; © Authenticated News/Hulton Archive/Getty Images, pp. 96–97; Courtesy Everett Collection, pp. 98, 100, 106, 113; © CBS Photo Archive/Hulton Archive/Getty Images, p. 99; © PBS/Courtesy Everett Collection, p. 101; Universal/The Kobal Collection, p. 103; Lucasfilm/20th Century Fox/The Kobal Collection, p. 104; MGM/The Kobal Collection, p. 105; © Museum of The City of New York/Hulton Archive/Getty Images, p. 107; © William Gottlieb/CORBIS, pp. 108–109; © Michael Ochs Archives/Getty Images, pp. 110, 114; © George Rose/Getty Images, p. 112; © H. Armstrong Roberts/Retrofile/Getty Images, pp. 116–117; © Popperfoto/Getty Images, p. 119; AP Photo/Kurt Strumpf, p. 121; AP Photo/jab, p. 123; © Larry C. Morris/New York Times Co./Hulton Archive/Getty Images, p. 125; AP Photo/Reed Saxon, p. 127 (top); AP Photo/Jim Bourdier, p. 127 (bottom); Courtesy Ronald Reagan Library, p. 130.

Front Cover: © Hulton Archive/Getty Images (top left); AP Photo/Nick Ut (top right); © Dirck Halstead/Liaison/Getty Images (bottom left); © Jesse-Steve Rose/The Image Works (bottom right).